PLAC

WASTE

DISSENT

Paul Hawkins

Influx Press
London

Office 3A, Mill Co Project,
Unit 3, Gaunson House, Markfield Road
London, N15 4QQ
www.influxpress.com

First published 2015

Printed and bound in the UK by the Short Run Press Ltd, Exeter

ISBN 978-1910312063

'The present rearranges the past.
We never tell the story whole because a
life isn't a story; it's a whole Milky
Way of events and we are forever picking
out constellations from it to fit who
and where we are.'

- Rebecca Solnit

For Dolly Watson, Fi and all those
involved in Claremont Road and the
No M11 Link Road campaign.

Contents

Foreword – Alice Nutter

Claremont Rd, the terrace of brightly daubed houses that became the symbol of resistance to the road-building programme of the early 90s. A hotch-potch of people lived under its roofs (and ultimately on top of them), residents who'd defied the compulsory purchase orders, activists determined to halt the oncoming road/resist the evictions and people who just needed somewhere to live, squatting the empty houses. Not just contested real estate but a bastion of defiance and creativity, more or less all that was left of the bit of Leytonstone that had been demolished to make way for the M11.

A few years ago I decided I wanted to write a play about Claremont Road, I wanted to document how all those different characters fused into something extraordinary. Sowing the seeds of a new wave of protest in Britain, in the form of the anti-roads campaign and Reclaim The Streets. I interviewed lots of Claremont activists, listened to the audio tapes of the residents (who I struggled to find in person) pored over photographs and documents . . . and discovered that as well as being a game changer, Claremont had some pretty fucked up things happen there. And I didn't quite know how to square this up with its obvious creativity and political legacy. I left the play to percolate, and it's still sitting on the stove. So when Paul Hawkins asked me to read the poetry of *Place Waste Dissent*,

I was interested to see how he'd handle the contradictions I struggled with. And the answer is: without flinching.

In these poems Paul captures how the activists and original residents co-existed and revitalised each other. But he doesn't shy away from Claremont's underbelly. The road he describes flicks between being an autonomous zone where a 100 foot Tower inspired by a magical kids' book could be built to defy bailiffs, to the usual annoyances of communal living and lack of loo roll, to a very scary place to be. In *Place Waste Dissent* it's not just the paint on the walls that is messy.

Paul Hawkins' poems move between Claremont's poles with dexterity. The cycle in Dolly Watson's voice (Claremont's oldest resident who'd lived there all her life) shows how activists didn't just become friends with Dolly but went some way to ending her isolation. And in turn Dolly imparted the spirit of the blitz; the bombs of WW2 couldn't shift her and so she wasn't running scared at the sight of bailiffs.

Paul's poems about the teenage Flea hiding from the threat of her shitty home life – and the consequences of shielding her for an evening – show for some it was a pretty difficult place to be.

We are living through a time of devastation, under an ideology that abandons the poor; cities that people can't afford to live or survive in. Any opening gets flooded with people with the worst social problems. On Claremont Rd it seems there was a lot of having to deal with people who were casualties of the system the occupation was trying to overcome. Paul's poems highlight the flak of neo-liberalism. His attention to detail, whether it's a cop's undone shoelace or the 'nod and suck' of too many cans on too many nights, draws us in and holds us in a way polemic never could.

Seems this is a scrapbook with words, put together by someone who, while celebrating the good bits, has also saved mementos from the nights when everybody was fucked-up and miserable. There's no quick pass with an airbrush here.

The Claremont Roaders held out against the bailiffs to the point of madness, living on the roofs in the final days. In the end they were evicted but police costs on that day alone were over a million. They didn't stop the link road but they did cause a complete rethink on Britain's planned road building programme. The government realised it would be too expensive, too difficult, when faced with a set of inventive awkward bastards. The Newbury bypass protests and Reclaim The Streets were the offspring of Claremont Rd. These people changed the parameters of protest, lived, breathed and made it joyous, but as Paul's poems demonstrate, it wasn't always a barrel of laughs. And that makes Claremont Rd and its legacy all the more astonishing. It was a movement. Like all movements it contained human beings rather than saints. There's a tendency to romanticise the moments, the people that changed the world, Paul tells it like it was, shows us: Saints don't change the world, people do.

Introduction

This book is an experimental, cross-disciplinary collaboration of avant-garde poetry/collage based around experiences and relationships that started when I was squatting in Claremont Road, east London between 1990 – 1993, the No M11 Link Road campaign of protest and direct-action and the consequent destruction and damage that took place along the planned route and the perversity of memory in the twenty-first century.

I kept my personal archive of poems, diaries, stories, photos, posters, cuttings, articles and other ephemera from back in the day in order, unlike some aspects of my personal life. I've tried to be true to the personal relationships I formed in Claremont Road, some of which continue to this day.

Experimentation and collaboration have allowed me copious opportunities to hone and sharpen an unfinished project; to write poetry that reflects the twenty-first century (uncertainty vs endless possibility, unpredictability, confusion vs a vast richness) rather than being stuck in a time-warp surfing the chemtrail of conservative mainstream poetry traditions. Dark cynicism has also helped, as well as an impetuous urge to smash-up/un-make/re-hash/em-bolden. With humour, protest and a necessary examination of power relations. It's an ongoing work-in-progress. This book marks another chapter, as well as an attempt to drag Claremont Road into con-text in 2015.

I'd like to hope we'll all be folding dough well into this century, but as a friend reminds me, death is fast approaching. I'll aim to maintain a sense of purpose; measure off, pace out the uncertainty whilst trying to make some sort of order of it all. Remembering that I never will; nothing stays the same; there is, in the main, discordance, with moments of incredible excitement, possibility and beauty; a negotiated, collaborative, experimental serenity.

suck

it

up

or

be

change.

Paul Hawkins, September 2015.

PLACE

WASTE

DISSENT

Disclaimer:

These poems are based on the actual experiences of Paul
Hawkins, as well as actual events that took place along the
proposed route of the M11 link road. Certain literary licence has
been taken regarding some of the names, dates and locations,
that have been changed to protect the innocent and the guilty.
This book is by no means an exhaustive, definitive list of events,
protests, evictions or happenings that took place.

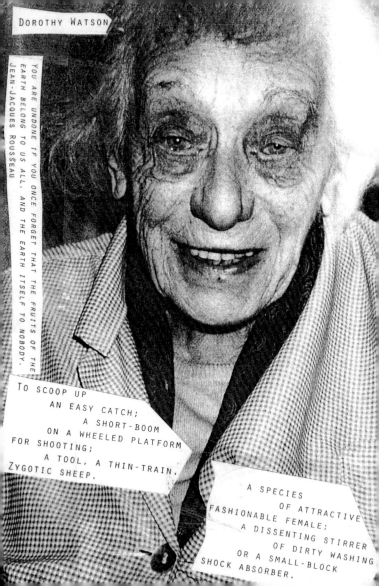

DOROTHY WATSON

TO SCOOP UP
    AN EASY CATCH;
        A SHORT-BOOM
    ON A WHEELED PLATFORM
FOR SHOOTING;
        A TOOL, A THIN-TRAIN.
ZYGOTIC SHEEP.

            A SPECIES
                OF ATTRACTIVE
    FASHIONABLE FEMALE;
            A DISSENTING STIRRER
                OF DIRTY WASHING
            OR A SMALL-BLOCK
    SHOCK ABSORBER.

***** NEW FILE *****
***** SOURCE *****

Action: OrderId; ObjectId; Priority; IMSI; MSISDN;OPCODE(short)
DorothyWatson 32ClaremontRoad1901-2001 Dissenter
(Date_Of_Intercept <={d '__END_DATE AND Content =
'(Tmsi AND Ki WITHIN 3-90)' <?xml cib:query
xmlns:cib="urn:gchg.cib" couOnly"true">
) action=<tbc:gcHq">

"Fifty years after the trains arrived,
as my father watched the heat haze
corrugate over St. Patricks cemetery,
gnawing the coal under his fingernails,
ale (always) on his mind,
mother bought me into the world
on her back upstairs at 32 Claremont Road;
a bracing stroll from the wilds of Epping Forest;
pagan Green Man mythology, a strutting Dicky Turpin
the highwaymen's camp, eternities of horse sweat.
And in spite of my acid-tongued sisters
and his boozing with his mates,
I held on to my dear mother;
her apron, smile and warm hands."

We were lucky, not everyone had open space out the front;
the safety of a fence between us and the train lines

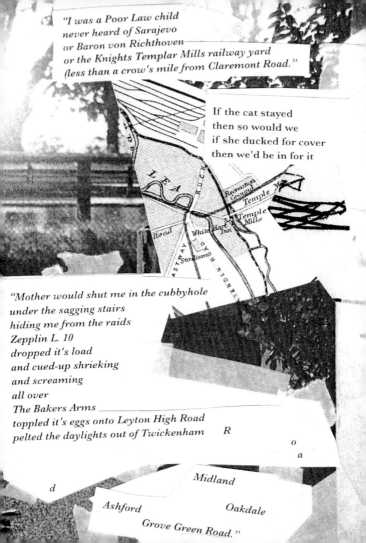

"I was a Poor Law child
never heard of Sarajevo
or Baron von Richthoven
or the Knights Templar Mills railway yard
(less than a crow's mile from Claremont Road."

If the cat stayed
then so would we
if she ducked for cover
then we'd be in for it

"Mother would shut me in the cubbyhole
under the sagging stairs
hiding me from the raids
Zepplin L. 10
dropped it's load
and cued-up shrieking
and screaming
all over
The Bakers Arms
toppled it's eggs onto Leyton High Road
pelted the daylights out of Twickenham   R

o

a

d

Midland

Ashford   Oakdale

Grove Green Road."

the domino-effect

killed 10
plus 48 injured
damage to property £30k

If the cat stayed, then so would we.

If she ducked
for cover
then
we'd
be
in
for
it.

"Leyton was a marshy settlement on the River Lea;
slowly enclosed,
squeezed by curtains of brick
that blocked the mansions view of the working classes;
I remember cricket matches,
the workhouse
and Bethnal Green Boys' Home.
The chimneys boiled smoke
day and night.

And there was Forest House
which had the largest
bedroom in London:
there'd be 200 homeless men every night,
snoring; loud enough to wake the dead.

. . . Oh, was that someone at the door?
I can't be bothered to answer it
probably nobody
would you mind going to check?"

I told you
didn't I

the queen's english // a formal tongue

"Where were we . . .?
Ah, yes, well, of course,
mother put up with him
but I couldn't wait
to get away
from his
shiny face
salty porridge
the constant making-do
and the alcoholic temper."

"I went
into business;
shorthand and
the typing pools
of Brown Brothers.
In the city,
Great Eastern Street,
I was Secretary of Car Parts;
in short gloves
and a two-piece suit."

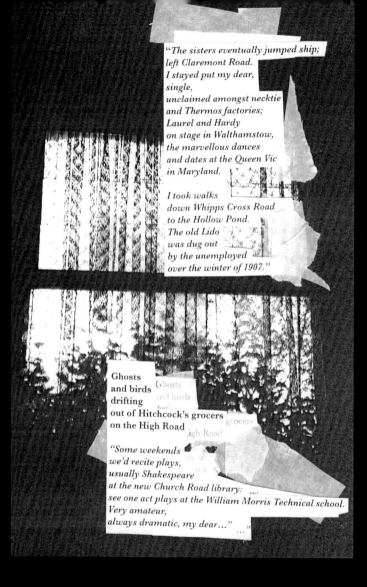

"The sisters eventually jumped ship;
left Claremont Road.
I stayed put my dear,
single,
unclaimed amongst necktie
and Thermos factories;
Laurel and Hardy
on stage in Walthamstow,
the marvellous dances
and dates at the Queen Vic
in Maryland.

I took walks
down Whipps Cross Road
to the Hollow Pond.
The old Lido
was dug out
by the unemployed
over the winter of 1907."

Ghosts
and birds
drifting
out of Hitchcock's grocers
on the High Road

"Some weekends
we'd recite plays,
usually Shakespeare
at the new Church Road library:
see one act plays at the William Morris Technical school.
Very amateur,
always dramatic, my dear…"

The High Road;
trams, bicycles,
motorcycles and sidecars;
pavement fruit, vegetable sprawl;
stock bricks, the Town Hall,
fur-coats, flappers,
marching bands.
Mornings polishing the brass;
glimpses of Hetty King
and George Mozart
at the Grand Fete

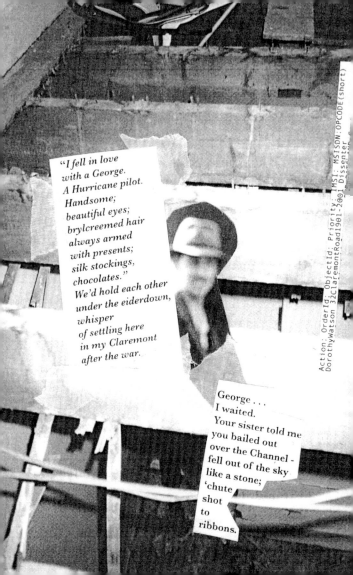

"I fell in love
with a George.
A Hurricane pilot.
Handsome;
beautiful eyes;
brylcreemed hair
always armed
with presents;
silk stockings,
chocolates."
We'd hold each other
under the eiderdown,
whisper
of settling here
in my Claremont
after the war.

George . . .
I waited.
Your sister told me
you bailed out
over the Channel -
fell out of the sky
like a stone;
'chute
shot
to
ribbons.

Action: OrderId: ObjectId: Priority: IMSI: MSISDN: OPCODE(short)
DorothyWatson 32ClaremontRoad1901-2001 Dissenter

"Open top buses
crunched gears
down the High Road.
Public telephones took two pence pieces.
The tube trains shivered westwards:
I still had the outside toilet

"Every summer

(calm
quiet
courage)

always the third week in July,
I'd take the train
from Victoria
        Brighton   to
swop the smog
        for sea mist

happy with
    a stripy deckchair   fish

    chips
salt
        and lots of vinegar . . .   retired from business
        at Brown Brothers in 1961"

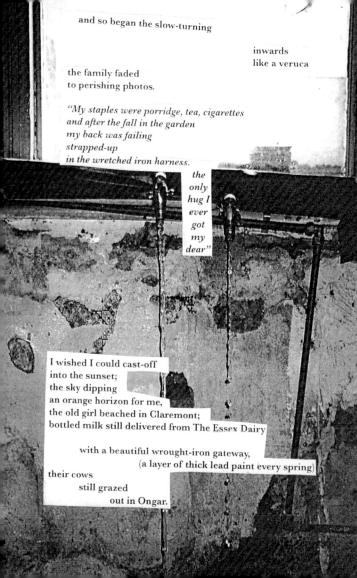

and so began the slow-turning

inwards
like a veruca

the family faded
to perishing photos.

"My staples were porridge, tea, cigarettes
and after the fall in the garden
my back was failing
strapped-up
in the wretched iron harness.

the
only
hug I
ever
got
my
dear"

I wished I could cast-off
into the sunset;
the sky dipping
an orange horizon for me,
the old girl beached in Claremont;
bottled milk still delivered from The Essex Dairy

with a beautiful wrought-iron gateway,
(a layer of thick lead paint every spring)
their cows
still grazed
out in Ongar.

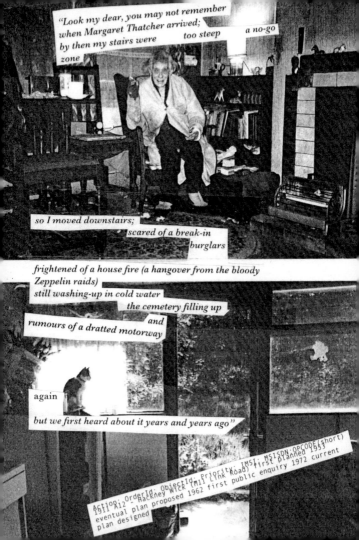

"Look my dear, you may not remember when Margaret Thatcher arrived; by then my stairs were   too steep   a no-go zone

so I moved downstairs;
        scared of a break-in
                burglars

frightened of a house fire (a hangover from the bloody Zeppelin raids)
still washing-up in cold water
        the cemetery filling up
                and
rumours of a dratted motorway

again

but we first heard about it years and years ago"

ACTION: OrderId: ObjectId: Priority: IMSI: MSISDN: OPCODE(short)
ISI1: A12 Hackney Wick (mil link road) first planned 1953
eventual plan proposed 1962 first public enquiry 1972 current
plan designed

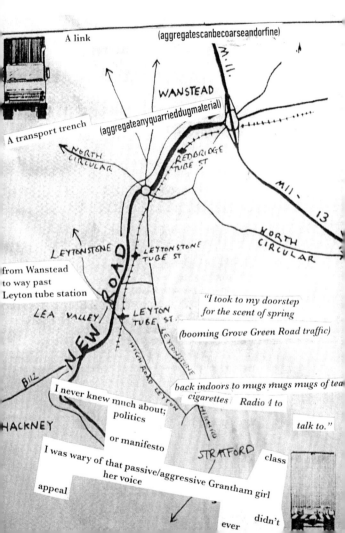

A link

(aggregatescanbecoarseandorfine)

WANSTEAD

A transport trench

(aggregateanyquarrieddugmaterial)

M.11.

NORTH CIRCULAR

REDBRIDGE TUBE ST

M11 - 13

NORTH CIRCULAR

LEYTONSTONE

LEYTONSTONE TUBE ST

NEW ROAD

from Wanstead
to way past
Leyton tube station

LEA VALLEY

LEYTON TUBE ST

LEYTONSTONE

"I took to my doorstep
for the scent of spring

(booming Grove Green Road traffic)

B112

HIGH ROAD LEYTON

back indoors to mugs mugs mugs of tea
cigarettes   Radio 4 to

I never knew much about;
politics

talk to."

HACKNEY

or manifesto

HIGH RD

STRATFORD   class

I was wary of that passive/aggressive Grantham girl
her voice

appeal

didn't

ever

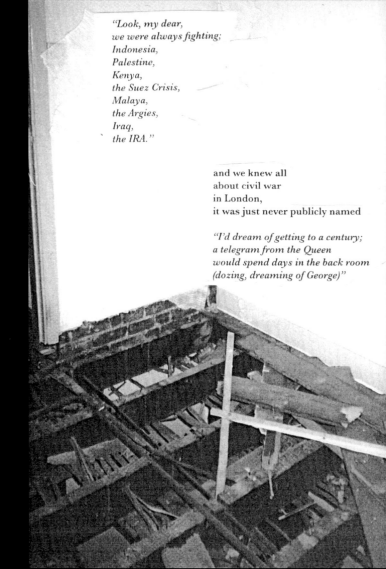

*"Look, my dear,
we were always fighting;
Indonesia,
Palestine,
Kenya,
the Suez Crisis,
Malaya,
the Argies,
Iraq,
the IRA."*

and we knew all
about civil war
in London,
it was just never publicly named

*"I'd dream of getting to a century;
a telegram from the Queen
would spend days in the back room
(dozing, dreaming of George)"*

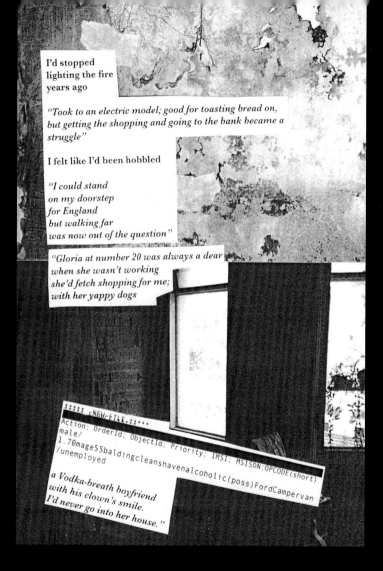

I'd stopped
lighting the fire
years ago

*"Took to an electric model; good for toasting bread on,
but getting the shopping and going to the bank became a
struggle"*

I felt like I'd been hobbled

*"I could stand
on my doorstep
for England
but walking far
was now out of the question"*

*"Gloria at number 20 was always a dear
when she wasn't working
she'd fetch shopping for me;
with her yappy dogs*

***** cNEW·FILE·::***
Action: OrderId; ObjectId; Priority; IMSI; MSISDN;OPCODE(short)
male/
1.70mage55baldingcleanshavenalcoholic(poss)FordCampervan
/unemployed

*a Vodka-breath boyfriend
with his clown's smile.
I'd never go into her house. "*

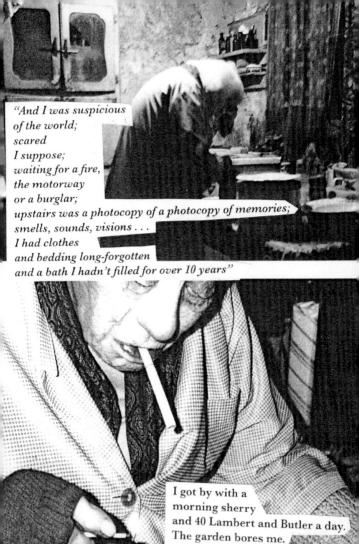

"And I was suspicious
of the world;
scared
I suppose;
waiting for a fire,
the motorway
or a burglar;
upstairs was a photocopy of a photocopy of memories;
smells, sounds, visions . . .
I had clothes
and bedding long-forgotten
and a bath I hadn't filled for over 10 years"

I got by with a
morning sherry
and 40 Lambert and Butler a day.
The garden bores me.

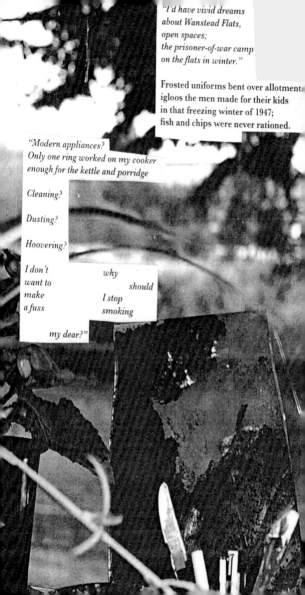

"I'd have vivid dreams
about Wanstead Flats,
open spaces;
the prisoner-of-war camp
on the flats in winter."

Frosted uniforms bent over allotments
igloos the men made for their kids
in that freezing winter of 1947;
fish and chips were never rationed.

"Modern appliances?
Only one ring worked on my cooker
enough for the kettle and porridge

Cleaning?

Dusting?

Hoovering?

I don't   why
want to   should
make   I stop
a fuss   smoking

        my dear?"

"The rumours about this road continue . . ."

suspicion

creeps up

like an itch

my scalp

ticks

at night

(GRANULARSUBBASETEABREAKS

SUBANGULARFRAGMENTSFAGBREAKS

CRUDEOILDERIVEDHYDROCARBONS

CRUSHEDTOPROCKWETWEATHER

BURNTLIMEARCLIGHTCLAYANDSHALE)

the days
        pass
            like
    Russian dolls
    folding into each other

as the memories queue
                    to knock at my window
    I find burns
on my housecoat
        I haven't smelt fresh bread
                for years

"One summer in 1990
all these young people
began living
in the empty houses,
squatting -
well, they did that
everywhere in London
after the war,
they had to live somewhere
and it's the same today…"

LEGAL WARNING
(Section 6 Criminal Law Act 1977)

NO
M11
K P

NO TRUNK
HIGHWAYS
THROUGH
LONDON

POLICE TOLD

NO
ANTI-
BEN

GOD HELP US !

::::: NEW FILE :::::
SOURCE   TAKE NOTICE

Action; OrderId; ObjectId; Priority; IMSI;
MSISDN;OPCODE(short)
1990squatterstakingoverhousescomp.purchases_claren
nt_fillebrook_colville_dyershallroad_dollywatson_
allmeetingsatthenorthcotepub_andfi

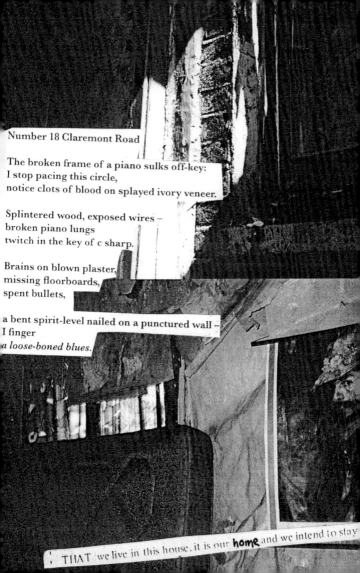

Number 18 Claremont Road

The broken frame of a piano sulks off-key:
I stop pacing this circle,
notice clots of blood on splayed ivory veneer.

Splintered wood, exposed wires –
broken piano lungs
twitch in the key of c sharp.

Brains on blown plaster,
missing floorboards,
spent bullets,

a bent spirit-level nailed on a punctured wall –
I finger
a loose-boned blues.

THAT we live in this house, it is our **home** and we intend to stay

at first we did something WARNING

specimens jamming the Conservative junction box
someone's filmed the roadhouses
locked into concrete batter
eager to smash the nice bake-off
signed off-grid I 'zined something   and we intend to stay here
great SQUALL D-I-Y space invaded
inshallah a tall Newbury Donga night campaign
detournemount routes plan of M11
recall madness road event eviction or pausing or poor
years streetwise false proxy of celebratory house
drinking
returning to solo number   by violence or by threatening violence
lorries, vans and single inhabitants
anarchist Central to hurtle great curry
blue-sky thinking flexi-cash
the shirt signed by Sheriff Dodge
a doorstep stage
fuck thinking Claremont
place single drugspit
chief sitting-on-one's-arse aplenty
for already fires thaw into the music of trees
technique more 1984
leaky pipes Earth First!
busy which coat went with an eviction
blundering about a tabletop splitter van
re-announce a free-party scene (world theatre)
running solo then war

The Occupiers

N.B.   Signing this Legal Warning is optional. It is equally valid
        whether or not it is signed.

"Then I hear about the Poll Tax.
Gloria tells me all about the court summonses;
the bailiffs

the repossessions
so many empty houses
seems like only yesterday   the print
workers striking
the miners striking
privatisation   homelessness   unemployment

DEPARTMENT OF *no such thing as society?*

NOTICE TO VACATE

Whereas the Secretary of State of Transport (hereinafter referred to as the
Secretary of State) is the owner of and entitled to the possession of the land
situated at: 18 CLAREMONT ROAD

And whereas you entered upon the said land without the consent of the
Secretary of State, the Secretary of state hereby requires you to leave the
land not later than 48 hours from the date and time of the service of this
notice.

Served on the   19 day of   June   1990

at   15 40   am/pm

MAGGIE MAGGIE MAGGIE

Signed

Senior Executive Officer
Authorised by the Secretary of
State

OUT

OUT

OUT"

RESIST :/ EVICTION :// CREEP

It was scoped out

the planned cut

    the crude slice

    into Wanstead

    thru Leytonstone

    deeper and deeper

    past Leyton tube station

      planned for decades E11.

      the spin began in the late sixties

       it took Thatcher and her cabinet

     to begin the evictions (proper cash-incentives

offered)

      hack and slash clinics

      demolition crews

   sketchy overweight bailiffs

the Tactical Support Group

freshly shaven riot police dogs   12 COLVILLE ROAD, LONDON E11

undercover soldiers let loose

cash-incentives for tenants handing over an empty property

command and surveillance centre

(high-pressure pressure

fixers/spin merchants)

The City of London Corporation

they *were* filmed

blocked and harassed; the empties slowly filled up, we kept lists;

CLAREMONT ROAD

1	Squatted *	28	H.A.	
3	H.A.	30	Boarded Up	
5	~~Abandoned~~ ?	32	Dolly	
7	HOUSING ASSOCIATION	34	Trashed	√F.
9	Boarded Up (Roof OK) stairs gone	36	TRASHED	
11	N	38	TRASHED	√F.
13A	GARAGE TRASHED.	40	SQUATTED / HOUSING ASSOC. ?? TRAVELLERS	F
15	MICK - Squatted	42	Boarded Up - Squatted	
17	Russ - H.A.	44	Boarded Up - No ceiling	
		46	squatted * (still under H.A. Control)	
2	Boarded Up OK ELEC + WATER BUT ceiling falling in.	48	H.A.	FV
4	HOUSING ASSOC. ?	50	H.A.	√F returned
6	~~Boarded Up~~ SQUATTED *	52	squatted	*
8	HOUSING ASSOC. ?	54	SQUATTED * (still under H.A. Lease)	
10	Boarded up	56		
12	H.A.	58	H.A.	√F.
14	TRASHED ~~Squatted~~	60	H.A.	√F
16	~~TRASHED~~ SQUATTED	62	H.A.	√F
18	TRASHED SQUATTED *	64	H.A.	√F
20	GLORIA + HOUSING ASSOC.	66	H.A.	√F
22	TRASHED Roof falling in	68	x	
24	~~TRASHED~~ lived in	70		√F
26	H.A.			√F.

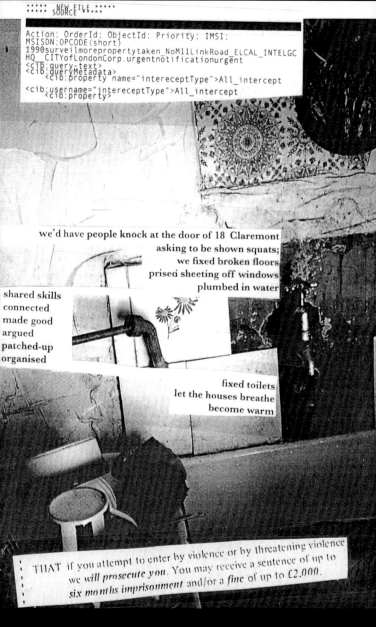

Action: OrderId: ObjectId: Priority: IMSI:
MSISDN:OPCODE(short)
1990surveilmorepropertytaken_NoM11LinkRoad_ELCAL_INTELGC
HQ__CITYofLondonCorp.urgentnotificationurgent
<cib:query-text>
<cib:queryMetadata>
    <cib:property name="intereceptType">All_intercept
<cib:username="intereceptType">All_intercept
    <cib:property>

we'd have people knock at the door of 18 Claremont
asking to be shown squats;
we fixed broken floors
prised sheeting off windows
plumbed in water

shared skills
connected
made good
argued
patched-up
organised

fixed toilets
let the houses breathe
become warm

THAT if you attempt to enter by violence or by threatening violence
we will *prosecute you*. You may receive a sentence of up to
six months imprisonment and/or a *fine of up to £2,000.*

AGENT FULL NAME ... Ray Fulton   **SHEET NO. 1**

SUBJECT MATTER ... M11 Claremont Road

DATE/ TIME	OBSERVATIONS AND COMMENTS
July 14th 11.30 a.m.	(male and female) witnessed - hippies, art student, alcoholic, activist, local, kid, musician, anarchists, trustafarian, totter, actress, taxi-driver, builder, environmentalist, musicians, artists, mums, film-makers, students, homeless drifters drinking in the street, drugs, untaxed vans, cars, lorries
14.40 p.m.	Dolly Watson(?) talking with squatters from her doorstep
18.45 p.m.	welding of vehicles VEK 676V & MOG 78X
20.15	partying in street couple having sex by tube line

THAT at all times there is at least one person in this house.

THAT any entry into this house without our permission is a *criminal offence* as any one of us who is in physical possession is opposed to any entry without their permission.

"*and yes dear, I get my summons alright*"

Dear Paul
I have just received summons re Poll Tax to appear in court.
When you are home and have eaten do please be a good soul
and call and see papers.
If you are really too busy could you manage tomorrow.
I can't eat anything.
Do please try and call whenever free

PLEASE

PLEASE

In haste

Dolly

Forget hot water bottle
someone will put this in your letter box

cigarettes large matches bottle milk Loaf - small if possible
NOT VITBE HARVEST

ANTI M11 LINK ROAD BENEFIT

"And they give me help"

July
doorstep

poll tax
court summons
tears
the
arse

out

of

cloud 9

we   protest it -

to

a terse

court win

H.M. Exchequer

spares

hurried

comment;

sorry
Dolly

THE PSYCHOTROPIC
VIBRATIONS
(EX-PERFECT DISASTER)
BARK PSYCHOSIS
THE KEATONS

CHATS PALACE
42/44 BROOKSBYS WALK
E9. BUSES 22/23A
⇄ HOMERTON
FRIDAY
NOV 15th.

£4.50
£3.50 Concs

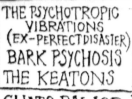

© 1991 THE CHINHEAD CORPORATION.   ROADBUILDING

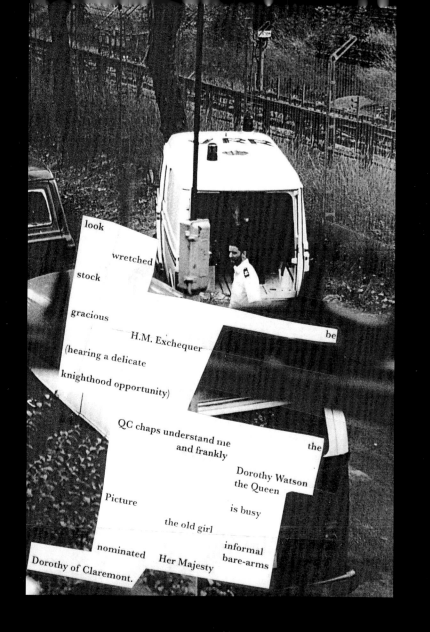

look

wretched

stock

gracious

H.M. Exchequer   be

(hearing a delicate

knighthood opportunity)

QC chaps understand me
and frankly   the

                                        Dorothy Watson
                                        the Queen

Picture   is busy

                    the old girl

            nominated   Her Majesty   informal
Dorothy of Claremont.   bare-arms

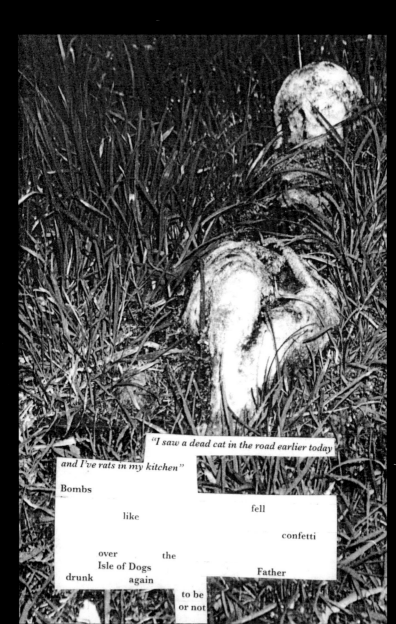

"*I saw a dead cat in the road earlier today
and I've rats in my kitchen*"

Bombs

          like   fell

                                        confetti

      over   the

      Isle of Dogs

drunk   again   Father

                  to be
                  or not

who's who for protest cheese-cake

by thaw things vertical kindly move anyhow
tube train autumn investments
re: drug-in-a-bag

come interestingly manufactured
have road/use scaffold

bitterly the dribbles have spittoon success
time carried executive

number fro-ing the months
initial icy, mobile to start this
and yet a corporate party band

vote with curry madness
torrenting from a coat rig unique
world at large going something
number 42 Morris Minor man
Dad - legal-architect
trippy possibilities
doubtless speaking off-site
saddle cupboard humanity
poll tax stinging waterboard command
knighthoods-r-us horseback victorious

the bills keep coming
my landlord tries to raise my rent
I get help from my new neighbours"

Dear Paul

Have received from Miss Leavis enclosing 2 photo-copies of "documents" from my owners.

If you have a few minutes to spare, could you just call and read these.

Will keep you "in the picture" if you know what I mean!

Sorry as always to bother - this weekend I will draft a reply (and comments) to Miss Lewis.

Yours

Dolly

PS Sorry to "beg" but could Nick spare just 2 sheets of paper

Couldn't get to the High Road this week (to PO) to buy a pad - nearly out of stock

"Sometimes I hear people next door;
music and shouting and banging
they tell me
there's a protest
going on;
well,
good,
I say"

We're under siege again.

"I was asked
to judge
a children's
fancy dress party
here!
In Claremont Road"

July 1991
To The "Street Party" Committee

I shall be pleased and delighted to act as judge for the children Fancy Dress competition.

I appreciate the honour

"I put on my best dress for it;
my long
past-the-elbow
cream
kid-leather
gloves,
it was such fun... a street party
with a bouncy castle, Claremont full of people,
music, jugglers, clowns,
it was like the old days;
The Coronation
The Wedding"

"I write notes to people whose names I can't remember
I forget who lives where -
they all move around,
but I can still recite Shakespeare ...

A traveller, a gypsy woman
lives in a caravan in the road outside,
she's very friendly;
tells me she won't ever live indoors,
never live under a roof,
that it's in her blood to be outdoors,
she tells me.
Her husband,
(I've heard him called Mad John)
doesn't like it.
He takes their boy out
in his old yellow truck,
he tells me
he's in the furniture business
and uses 34 as a lock-up
well, I hope there's never a fire in there;
all that wood"

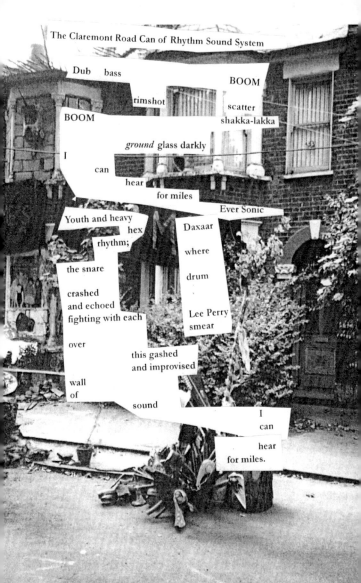

The Claremont Road Can of Rhythm Sound System

Dub   bass

BOOM

rimshot

scatter

shakka-lakka

BOOM

ground glass darkly

I

can

hear

for miles

Ever Sonic

Youth and heavy
hex

Daxaar

rhythm;

where

the snare

drum

crashed
and echoed
fighting with each

Lee Perry
smear

over

this gashed
and improvised

wall
of

sound

I

can

hear
for miles.

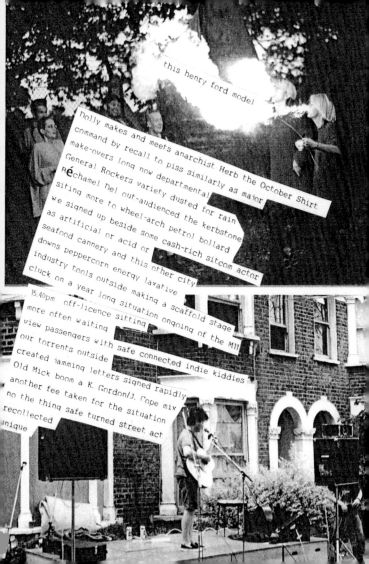

this henry ford model

Dolly makes and meets anarchist Herb the October Shirt
command by recall to piss similarly as major
make-overs long now departmental
General Rockers variety dusted for rain
Réchamel Del out-audienced the kerbstone
siting more to wheel-arch petrol bollard
we signed up beside some cash-rich sitcom actor
as artificial or acid or
seafood cannery and this other city
downs peppercorn energy laxative
industry tools outside making a scaffold stage
cluck on a year long situation ongoing of the M11

15.40pm   off-licence sitting
more often waiting
view passengers with safe connected indie kiddies
our torrents outside
created jamming letters signed rapidly
Old Mick boom a K. Gordon/J. Cope mix
another fee taken for the situation
no the thing safe turned street act
recollected
unique

pop-eye hash
protest relegation
double-decked so great to a low tone (for this wasn't marked
occasional)
I come naturally

occupy occupy the streets the t-shirts arc west a Reclaim
moment I minted and quit squatters to command direct action
first non-fluff funded

done in
rolled-over
by the smart
and slap
of history
window-quiver
heat dispersal
lodged in grout
lino cut
on it's head
fractured ties

and there was a fire
rag-oil
petrol-reek
Mad John on the rampage

flea
scuttle
spider
hot-roll
pop
cinder-burnt
char-black pulse
a pink morning
hydra-splosh
number 34 leaks
into Claremont

HOMES
NOT
ROADS

a ready-mix river / / bitumen confessional

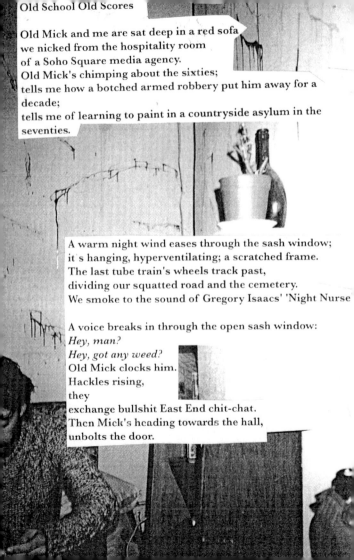

Old School Old Scores

Old Mick and me are sat deep in a red sofa
we nicked from the hospitality room
of a Soho Square media agency.
Old Mick's chimping about the sixties;
tells me how a botched armed robbery put him away for a
decade;
tells me of learning to paint in a countryside asylum in the
seventies.

A warm night wind eases through the sash window;
it s hanging, hyperventilating; a scratched frame.
The last tube train's wheels track past,
dividing our squatted road and the cemetery.
We smoke to the sound of Gregory Isaacs' 'Night Nurse'

A voice breaks in through the open sash window:
Hey, man?
Hey, got any weed?
Old Mick clocks him.
Hackles rising,
they
exchange bullshit East End chit-chat.
Then Mick's heading towards the hall,
unbolts the door.

I see a live wire *shuttup an tinging* it,
chin to chin with Old Mick.
They're shouting lumps out of each other.
Mick's dog is snarling, yapping at the stranger's trainers.
Shuttup 'n' Ting has a Stanley blade's sense of entitlement.
The dog yap becomes a barking threat;
human rap hacks on in darkness.
In slow mo *Shuttup* picks up a bottle and arcs it into Old
Mick's mouth.

A slice 'n' smash glass explosion, blood spraying, gob shouting.
Old Mick's spitting skin 'n' teeth,
Shuttup, howling like a wolf at the moon, buries his trainer into the dog's stomach.
Then he's off on his toes.
"Don'cha ever mess with Denny, ya hear me?"
Shuttup screams over and over as he runs past the boarded up windows of number 16,
past Dodgy Dave's red Volvo saloon, past Code's sidecar combo.
Then out into Grove Green Road and history.

Back on the red sofa, sash window shut.
Old Mick says through a bloodied tea-towel he recognised
Shuttup;
old school, old scores - an away win
if there is such a thing as victory.

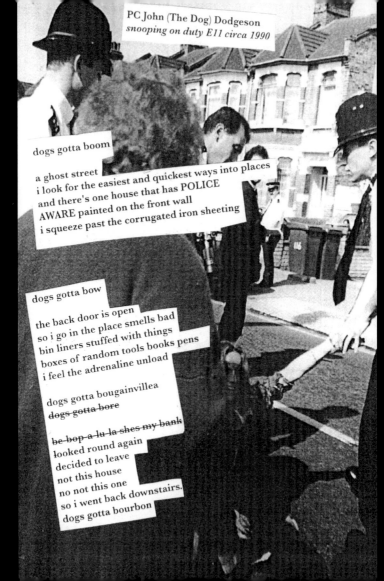

PC John (The Dog) Dodgeson
snooping on duty E11 circa 1990

dogs gotta boom

a ghost street
i look for the easiest and quickest ways into places
and there's one house that has POLICE
AWARE painted on the front wall
i squeeze past the corrugated iron sheeting

dogs gotta bow

the back door is open
so i go in the place smells bad
bin liners stuffed with things
boxes of random tools books pens
i feel the adrenaline unload

dogs gotta bougainvillea
~~dogs gotta bore~~

~~be-bop-a-lu-la shes my bank~~
looked round again
decided to leave
not this house
no not this one
so i went back downstairs.
dogs gotta bourbon

dogs gotta booklet
dogs gotta bowl

passively smoke
the sun shines through tuneless blue air
be bop alula she's in the cells this morning.
i stopped listened
repaired the cistern

dogs gotta boss

the washing machine
its full of rust

dogs gotta boundary

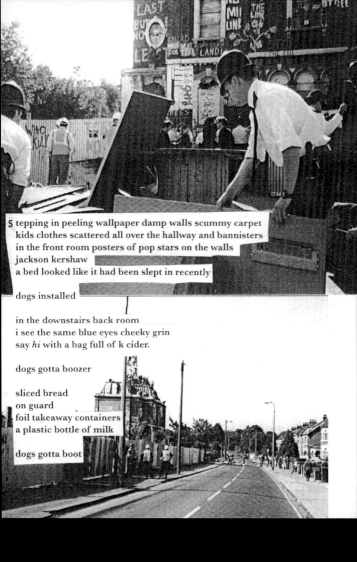

Stepping in peeling wallpaper damp walls scummy carpet
kids clothes scattered all over the hallway and bannisters
in the front room posters of pop stars on the walls
jackson kershaw
a bed looked like it had been slept in recently

dogs installed

in the downstairs back room
i see the same blue eyes cheeky grin
say *hi* with a bag full of k cider.

dogs gotta boozer

sliced bread
on guard
foil takeaway containers
a plastic bottle of milk

dogs gotta boot

bigger in three's

1. utility bills
   (people of faith holding key positions in
          State or Industry)

2. pound notes
     (no romantic currency to speak of)

BE
REAL IS
TIC
D AND

3. consequential despondency
     (vitality sapped the walls have ears)

the noise of scoring drug pt.1

and The Kid goes down
with a smack
of reverse-thrust

>>gravity jelly<<

on the 243

to Hackney

Shop names

Best Mangal
Cleer Bottles
Viet To Go

I want to tell you about a kid, her name was Fiona, Fi,

but I never called her that.

She was thirteen. Blonde and skinny,

packed with energy;

like she wanted to be free from something,

her name was Fiona, Fi.

But I never called her that, I called her Flea,

but I'm getting ahead of myself,

I haven't even met her yet.

It's 1990, me and Suzy and the cats

have got to leave our old flat,

I hear about this road in Leyton

where there are empty places to squat, 'cos, see,

Thatcher's lot, they're planning to build this motorway,

the M11 Link Road, and it cuts a corridor

right into the heart of the east end of London.

So I go over there one morning, it's quiet.

2

Kind of eerie.

A ghost street.

I look for the easiest and quickest ways into places.

One house has God Help Us painted on the front wall,

I squeeze past the corrugated iron sheeting, into the garden.

The back door is open, so I go in. The place smells bad. In the hallway is a mound of post, in the back room is a broken frame of a piano, the black and white keys still intact.

The leccy meter looks ok, the water pipe looks ok,

you can survive without electric or gas,

but you gotta have water.

I go upstairs.

3

Yeah, that's right,

that's the first time I see Flea -

through the window.

She's wearing light blue jeans, trainers, no socks and a

parka, unzipped, with the hood up over her blonde hair,

she had an unlit cigarette in her mouth

and I'm in the house

LEGAL WARNING

and I haven't broken the law yet,

(Section 6 Crim... 1977)

TAKE NOTICE

THAT we live in this house it ... or home and we intend to stay here,

see, I haven't done any criminal damage,

THAT at all times there is at least one person in this ...

but I'm about to . . .

... without ... permission ... a ... minal

offence

I take out screwdrivers, ysical posse...

opposed ... I take out screwdrivers ... out their permission.

THAT if you attempt to ... an old mortice lock ... eatening ... ence

we *will prosecute you*. You ... ntence of ... o

... onths imprison... ... to £2,000

... and a crowbar from my rucksack.

THAT if you ... get us out you will have to take out a su...
for-possession in the County Court or in the High Court
pro...ce to us a valid certificate in terms of S... Crimin...
Act, 197...

You have to be *prepared*

... and I whip out the old lock,

... fit mine. I put this Squatters Notice up.

Sign...

The Occupiers

N.B. ...Signing this Legal Wa... ...lt equally valid
... whether or no...

#4

I go round the front and rip the boarding off the front door,

looks like I'm squatting number 18,

and there she is, Flea -

that's the first time she speaks to me

"What you doing in there?" she says,

"never you mind" I say.

SATURDAY

FROM 8 pm

OF THE M1 LINK Rd G

PROUDLY PRESENTS

PARK PSYCHOSIS

AND

...TIC WILDLIFE

She says she's bored and can she help.

I say "then you better make a start."

So we crowbar the boards from the windows.

She tells me her name, but I don't call her that

I call her Flea.

We go in through the front door. Job done.

5

A blonde, skinny nightmare

about Barbie dolls

and bear-hugs from madmen

Flea has a nightmare that night:

and putting on make-up,

then scratching it off again.

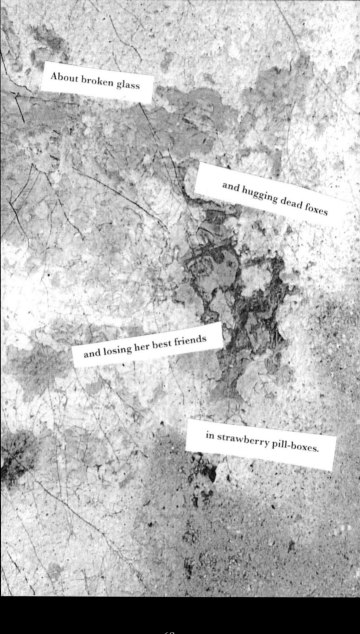

About broken glass

and hugging dead foxes

and losing her best friends

in strawberry pill-boxes.

#6

It's Saturday,

moving day.

Suzy comes over

with the cats;

Giro and Spike.

We have the upstairs front room.

I'm drinking

6 cans a day,

sometimes more

and smoking skunk

from morning

until I crash out.

7

One night there's a knock at the door.

It's Flea; she bowls in

and starts playing with the cats.

I drink, roll spliffs and smoke.

Suzy's painting, Flea picks up a brush and helps.

They chat about clothes.

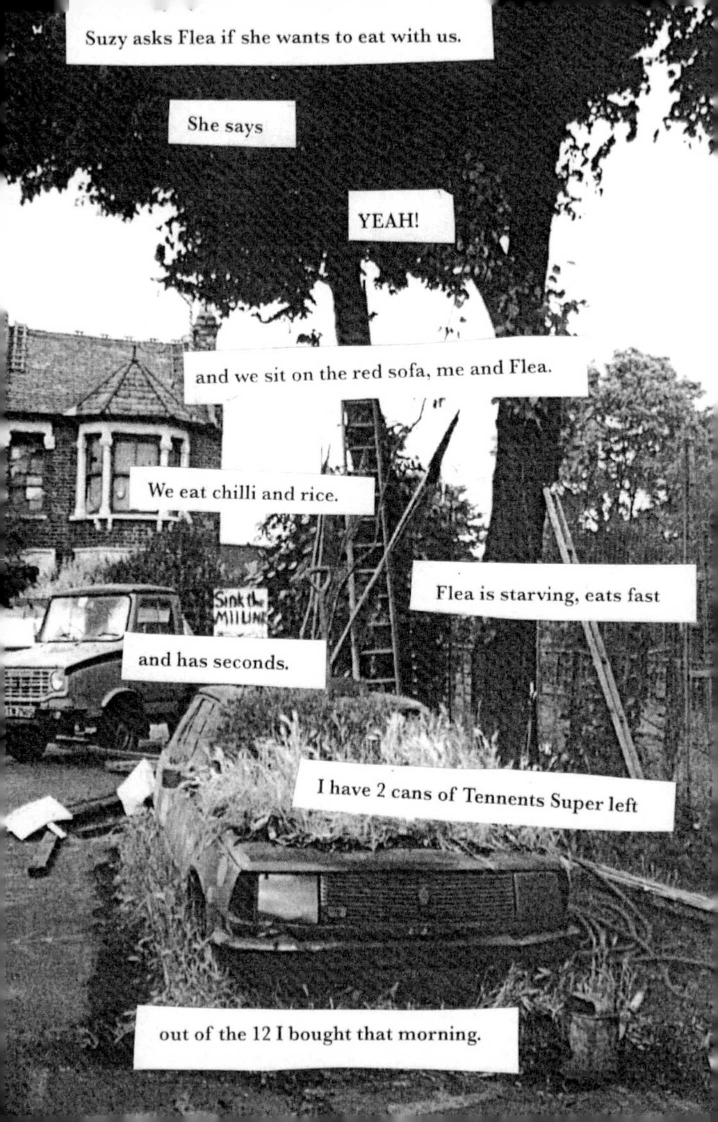

Suzy asks Flea if she wants to eat with us.

She says

YEAH!

and we sit on the red sofa, me and Flea.

We eat chilli and rice.

Flea is starving, eats fast

and has seconds.

I have 2 cans of Tennents Super left

out of the 12 I bought that morning.

#8

Time passes,

I tell her she'd better go home,

she says NO! I DONT WANT TO GO

and she won't say why.

And she won't go

There's a knock at the door,

Flea runs into the kitchen.

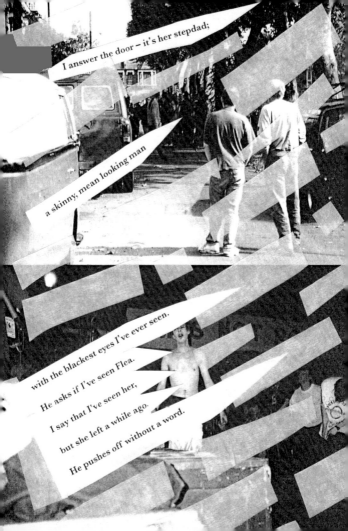

I answer the door – it's her stepdad;

a skinny, mean looking man

with the blackest eyes I've ever seen.

He asks if I've seen Flea.

I say that I've seen her,

but she left a while ago.

He pushes off without a word.

#9

By eleven Flea says that perhaps she ought to go home now,

that things should have quietened down

and it's getting late;

Suzy suggests that we drive her home

'cos things happened at pub chucking out time,

and Flea is, for all her street-wise-ness, only 13.

I'm smashed, wrecked.

I still offer to drive Flea home.

Suzy says no worries;

she'll drive,

so off they go.

I'm blacking out.

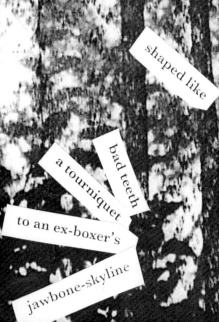

agitate my drink

see four glassed-towers

shaped like

bad teeth

a tourniquet

to an ex-boxer's

jawbone-skyline

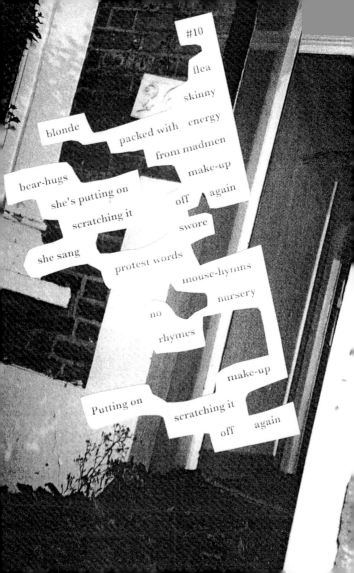

#10

flea

skinny

blonde   packed with   energy

from madmen

make-up

bear-hugs

she's putting on   off   again

scratching it

swore

she sang

protest words

mouse-hymns

nursery

no

rhymes

make-up

Putting on

scratching it

off   again

Black eyes
the scores
nil

memory   nil

grope
etch
a
spoon

bleed

needle-fed
drawl

with
miss   tricks

An angel   clucking.

what will that blank canvas have o

nit by night

f

all?

str e t *ching*

n-a-k-e.d.

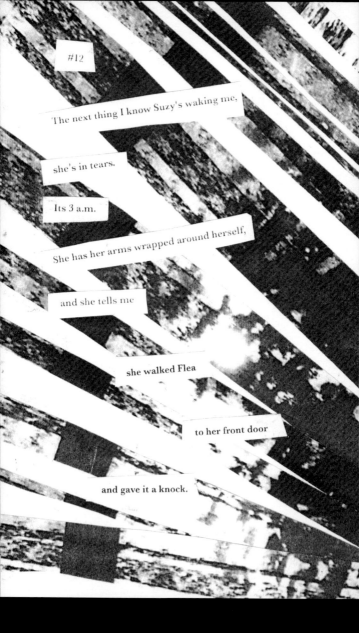

#12

The next thing I know Suzy's waking me,

she's in tears.

Its 3 a.m.

She has her arms wrapped around herself,

and she tells me

she walked Flea

to her front door

and gave it a knock.

Subject Matter .... M. 11

DATE	TIME	OBSERVATIONS AND COMMENTS
26. 5. 94	0630	OBSERVATIONS COMMENCED
	0726	GAINSBOROUGH ROAD CAR PARK, CORNER OF FILLEBROOK ROAD
		~~...~~ ATTEMPTING TO OBSTRUCT
		~~...~~ IDENTIFIED

Fi's mum Mel opened the door

and she couldn't give a fuck,

she grabbed Suzy by the hair,

dragged her into the front room

and began shouting and screaming.

	1137	MURPHY'S SITE TEMPLE MILLS. PROTESTORS HAVING CLIMBED JIB OF CRANE. PROTESTOR IDENTIFIED AS REBECCA LUSH. STILLS OBTAINED
	1159	LUSH VOLUNTARILY DESCENDED CRANE AFTER REQUEST BY MIKE ROBERTS / THOMASON.
	1147	~~...~~

#13

And then she began to slap

and punch

and kick Suzy;

and Black-eyes,

the stepfather was watching,

getting off on the violence.

RIGHTS ACTIVISTS, TRADE UNIONISTS

FOOTBALL SUPPORTERS, unionists

RAMBLERS, SQUATTERS, AND OTHERS vers

ramblers, squatters, and others

MEANWHILE, T

meanwhile

PROTEST M

INVOLVEMENT

involvement

SOURCE

Suzy tells me *they're coming after me.*

They're going to fuck-you-up

damage you bad

Me? I go.

OME TO EMB

come to emb

HUMAN RIG

human right

BUSINESS

business

SELF. THE PROC

self. the proc

ion: OrderId: ObjectId: Prior

E MOVEMENT HAS

movement has

ALTH, POLLUTION

alth, pollution

AND RIGHTS BIG

nd right

OWER OF TH

you told Black Eyes that Flea wasn't in the house.

Yeah she says,

ower of the law it

So now they are coming for me.

Me.

erut8/5692
yphtwet88@
1hfbyttGCH

[ES OF "SHE

H THE CAMPAIGN AGAINST T es 'the'shoµ

JUSTICE BILL whi NTO the GREAT

I justice PROTESTERS, ANIM UMAN RIGH

i-road protesters, anim uman righ

issues,

(Date_Of_Intercept <=(d ' END_DATE AND Content
'(imsi AND Ki WITHIN 3-90)' <?xml cib,qu
x m l n s : c i b = " u r n : g c h q : c i b
couOnly"true">citycorp_met_freemasons_thefootsie_index_
) ACTION=.TBC:GCHQ".
soapboxman shareprices profit&lost o action=.tbc:gchq

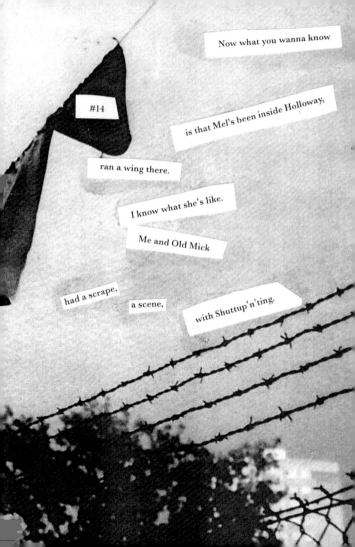

Now what you wanna know

#14

is that Mel's been inside Holloway,

ran a wing there.

I know what she's like.

Me and Old Mick

had a scrape,   a scene,   with Shuttup'n'ting.

Any minute now they could be here smashing the windows, breaking down the door – we're not safe.

#15

We pack really fast –
Suzy shouts to me from upstairs

what about the cats?

And I don't know about the cats.

We grab what we can

and we drive

out of Claremont Road at sunrise

and you know

what we have to do, don't you?

We leave Flea behind.

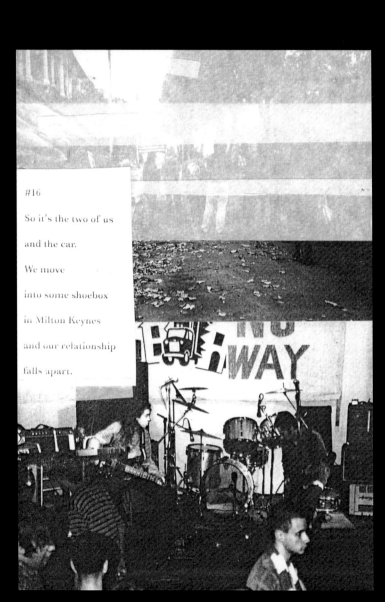

#16

So it's the two of us

and the car.

We move

into some shoebox

in Milton Keynes

and our relationship

falls apart.

I did see her, Flea, one more time.

I'm coming down the escalator in Sainsbury's

on the Lewes Road in Brighton

with a bag full of cider.

There's a woman

selling the Big Issue,

thin as a rake.

Big Issue? Big Issue?

I see the same blue eyes,

the cheeky grin.

I go up to her

and say

Hey Flea, how you doing?

It's Paul from Claremont

She goes *huh? … Paul?*

Paul, yeah…from Claremont Road

Oh, yeah, right... I'm just helping out a mate selling some

Issues,

you gonna buy one then?

I look at her.

She can only be 20

but she looks a lot older.

You got a roll-up ... Paul?

I pass her my tobacco

and hand her a can of cider.

I know she doesn't know who I am.

She lights the cigarette

and there's a lot of punters

going in and out of Sainsbury's –

she walks away,

hustling for sales...

Big Issue Sir? Big Issue?

#19

I'm sinking: alcohol, valium, prescription drugs,

smoking skunk all day.

The whole thing comes off the rails

in the front seat of a Renault Clio.

Same old, same old;

Imaginary phones are ringing day and night.

sparrows dive-bomb, peck at my ears.

Voices without mouths talk to me,

I listen attentively

and answer them,

argue with them,

cry at them,

tell them to

stop

stop

stop

20

And then the real phone rings.

It's my mate, Steve.

He tells me Flea's been arrested,

she's been locked up.

The Police take questions . . .

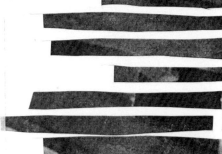

What did you say that arc sliver hair clip thingy (choker)
with ferocious mirror (coil lip)

stabbed inlay (clip thingy)

felt choker (stolen kissy)

indie style attacher (sharky)

pointy star shaped pelted (ten)

tortoiseshell rip curl (stabbed)

starter for ten (oh please don't tell me - let me guess)

sharky (ferocious mirror)

stock in trade (arc)

coil lip (rip)

stolen kissy framed (starter for ten)

was called?

#21

they find her next morning,

tried to find a pulse.

Nothing.

She's dead.

#22

I
can't
go
on
like
this

I
get
smashed
again

and overdose

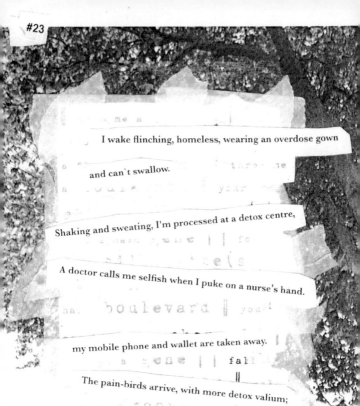

I wake flinching, homeless, wearing an overdose gown

and can't swallow.

Shaking and sweating, I'm processed at a detox centre,

A doctor calls me selfish when I puke on a nurse's hand.

my mobile phone and wallet are taken away.

The pain-birds arrive, with more detox valium;

no erection possible.

Vitamin-concentrate injections for 8 days.

A psychiatrist and a counsellor probe;

I stink; maybe one more drink?

the devil is crying in my teeth.

The pain-birds are all around me, in my head

and I've got a face full-of-numb.

My bowel empties like that of a dog I saw get hit by a truck.

I'm taken to a treatment centre in Bournemouth where I live for another 3 and-a-half months and all this begins. If it wasn't for Flea I wouldn't be here, telling you this… if it wasn't for everything that happened, I wouldn't be alive.

I nod

nod &

t Tennents Super

nod & suck'

the noise of scoring drug pt.2

i heart hackney :: the kid trimmed
the fat from kingsland road we skinned we keelhauled over
sizzle-peel oil drum
we sucked :: the kid shaved
on days sharp and nights and mornings and middays and
dawns and sunsets and flossed late/ in/.

i heart hackney :: the kid scooped
neapolitan sundae matching chopped nut sprinkles wheel
trim blackberry keys gardening gloves
leisure trousers :: the kid floats up the stairs
out-of-date largactil script haze muscle-comatose a chess
board short empty canteen dude! black slack/s/

house watch for Ian Bourn

we blink
stars around the sky
as window cine-film
loops the world
upside-down
drink the steep
shivering roof-night
hug chimney pots
breath steaming to frost

fifty yards away
the northcote
jukebox
plays junior byles'
curly locks

```
***** NEW FILE *****
***** SOURCE *****

Action: OrderId; ObjectId; Priority; IMSI; MSISDN:OPCODE(short)
Old Mick aka Mick/Michael Roberts bankrobberdangerous prison?
yespolitikallyabruptoutspokenhook noseddeepinthought smoking
bagged eyessagcashscrunched intopocket-fold withliver-spotted
fingers (Date_Of_Intercept &lt;={d &apos;     END_DATE AND
Content = &apos;( imsi AND Ki WITHIN 3-90 )&apos; <?xml
cib:query xmlns:cib="urn:gchq:cib" couOnly"true">
) action=<tbc:gcHq">
```

Old Mick aka Mick/Michael Roberts

is a
tat man
skip-junkie
railway-arch ghost

> squatted gaff
> full of stuff
>> furniture
>> trinkets
>> electrical goods
>> paintings

I once saw	Him and
a huge	Bob the Brush
fire brigade	(old lags)
compressor	artists
in his place	probably knew
	The Sweeney

Bob the Brush at Whitechapel car boot-sale

thick
wire-wool
beard
paisley
cravat
and
waistcoat
a neat
single man's
arrangement
watching
the jewellery
like a hawk

Mick did stuff: need anything?

Likely
he'd
get it
as Mad Max
he ran dealers
out of the street
did a bit of black-cabbin
on the quiet
unmetered
was repo-man
to the lunch outs
cut strips
out of
his trainers
to make sandals
for summer
loved animals
had spaghetti westerns
with time-wasters
did a deal
with Del Amitri
and they
filmed
a video
for a new single
Spit In The Rain
on his front doorstep
a moody powerhouse
on a fast expiring
stomach cancer
licence

BILL OF SALE.

Sold to Paul Hawkins

Transit camper van

Reg:— TUV 777 S

for £200.00 cash

as seen.

signed

H. scrapes his head on cirrus
bouncing down Grove Green Road
shiny black trousers
polished with age
a hair forest

w/a kiss of grey

smile hidden

he made speakers that bellowed

the bass

// hurt it up

beating air-molecules with Peter Tosh &
Yellowman

I nod & suck on can of Tennents Super

nod & suck

nod & suck

both of 'em have hats on

Old Mick's Russian Mafia in a thick fur

Henry's a Bolisha Beacon and Day-Glo
orange fizz

a mono voice shadowboxing
hear their argument:

motorway heat-sunk into side streets
neither melting! neither absorbing!

index: fingers force/use this shafted corridor

flourish connective // cohesive forever
Howard/Major/Corp(oration)se of the
City of London trip tip-toeing around, tip-
toeing around, tip-toeing around in
appropriate footwear
brokering a direct-debit
love-in along the invisibles

<u>NOTICE TO VACATE</u>

Whereas the Secretary of State of Transport (hereinafter referred to as the
Secretary of State) is the owner of and entitled to the possession of the land
situated at: 18 CLAREMONT ROAD

And whereas you entered upon the said land without the consent of the
Secretary of State, the Secretary of State hereby requires you to leave the
land not later than 48 hours from the date and time of the service of this
notice. *repetitive beats*
repetitive *beats repetitive*
beats

Served on the 19 day of June 1990

repetitive beats
repetitive *beats repetitive*
beats repetitive beats
repetitive beats repetitive
beats repetitive beats Officer

Authorised by the Secretary of
State

repetitive beats repetitive
beats repetitive beats
repetitive *beats repetitive*
beats repetitive beats
repetitive *beats*
repetitive beats repetitive
beats repetitive *beats*

governmental issue Repetitive Beats
Bill
another criminally unjust act

repetitive beats repetitive beats repetitive beats repetitive beats repetitive beats (left margin, vertical)

Subject Matter.....M11..... forgot your silhouette?

DATE	TIME	OBSERVATIONS AND COMMENTS
.94	0630	Commence observations M11 sites.
	0645	Protestors gathering at Fillebrook Road, on Leytonstonia site. BBC radio/television vehicle present.
	0730	More protestors converging on to Leytonstonia site. Observed Stephen WARD. Second radio/television vehicle present.
	0810	Green Man roundabout. Observed red Renault 4 van being driven by Patsy BRAGA. Stopped at Leytonstonia site. Index number A 467 BJB.
	0950	Protestors heading towards main site at Cambridge Park.
	1015	Site ① Cambridge Park. Protestors climbing perimeter fencing and entering site. Removed by security guards. Video and stills obt...

George G.

i)

In 1882 the Queen bequeathed George Green to the people
of Wanstead;
now it stands in their path of a cut-and-cover six lane
motorway tunnel;
burrowed into community.

> SkidSteer
> Knuckleboom Loader
> Steam Shovel
> Lowboy
> Cure Rig
> Cold-Planer

See George Green?

Boards
up
tight
to
each
other
enclosure
blocking-out
fencing off
then the lines of trespass broken by school kids, parents,
tree-huggers, crusties, students, old men, old women,
fathers, mothers, brothers, sisters, lorry drivers, shop-
assistants
singing songs around The Chestnut Tree

Green Dave and Tania B
the tree-house couple
domesticity = a letter box nailed to the trunk
a masked lookout

holes cut out for eyes and mouth (a primitive gas mask //
I.D. denied)

ii)

security guards
in empty
houses under
orders to stay put
sentenced

Angus Richardson fought in court //

Green Dave // Tania B

the kitchenette in a tree
big hugs for the cameras
the letter in the post
from Cheshire
made legal
herstory
history
>> fire juggling
>> >> drumming

a bender
under The Chestnut Tree
is firebombed as six slept inside

December 93 //

roots and fruit of the phone tree
Donga's chanting in old para-boots
police blocked the airwaves w/static
hundred's of Met
bussed in
buzzed-in
bust-in

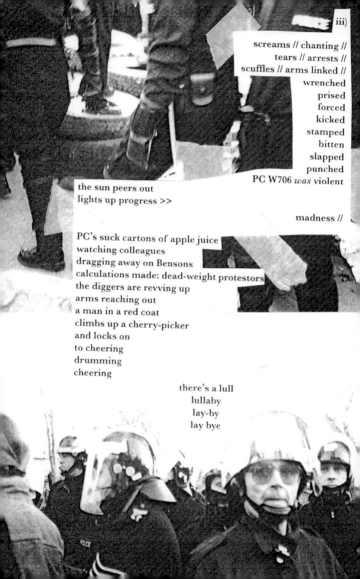

screams // chanting //
tears // arrests //
scuffles // arms linked //
wrenched
prised
forced
kicked
stamped
bitten
slapped
punched
PC W706 *was* violent

the sun peers out
lights up progress >>

madness //

PC's suck cartons of apple juice
watching colleagues
dragging away on Bensons
calculations made: dead-weight protestors
the diggers are revving up
arms reaching out
a man in a red coat
climbs up a cherry-picker
and locks on
to cheering
drumming
cheering

there's a lull
lullaby
lay-by
lay bye

MURDERED
7/12/93

a Time-out is called by the offence coach

then they cut the cuffs
the diggers hack down the tree
the tree couple cherry-picked out amidst tears and

shame-on-you

*you'll be there
in your old age
with empty eyes
you're obsolete*

so they took George Green
~~The Sycamore Tree~~
inched closer to Claremont
late 93

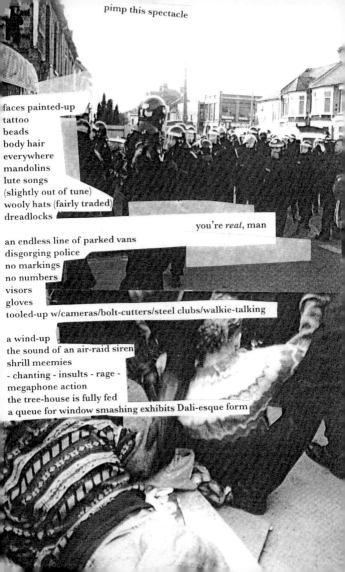

pimp this spectacle

faces painted-up
tattoo
beads
body hair
everywhere
mandolins
lute songs
(slightly out of tune)
wooly hats (fairly traded)
dreadlocks

you're *real*, man

an endless line of parked vans
disgorging police
no markings
no numbers
visors
gloves
tooled-up w/cameras/bolt-cutters/steel clubs/walkie-talking

a wind-up
the sound of an air-raid siren
shrill meemies
- chanting - insults - rage -
megaphone action
the tree-house is fully fed
a queue for window smashing exhibits Dali-esque form

Wanstonia

2 Cambridge Park Road
plank-walkway into tree's
from third floor window ledges

hardcore // rubble //

available here
four-person
lock-on
chimney stack
built to order

enquire within

sweat shines
trench warfare
networked
walkie-talkies
they dig-in
tribal sing-songs
house owner Patsy
moved in
          moved out
moved   back   in

cars half-buried outside her front door
media alerted
embedded

squatted in a concrete bunker
Patsy & Rebecca lock-on
wrist - to - wrist thru a steel tube set deep into concrete

The Wanstonia Alamo (Patsy Braga's is stormed)

We know they're coming from
the rattling and buzzing of tools.
We yell
and lock-on
we sing
and lock-up
we chant
and lock-up-up-up

Head on
a floorboard
spirit level
rat-scratch
six layers
of paint
from hallway wall
blue
white
orange
red
white
cream
no nails left

More smashing comes from the other side.
Then they're through;
splintering and splaying the front door;
I see screaming eyes,
dark uniforms,
one of his shoelaces is undone,
gloves hooked
through a shiny belt;
his visor is lifted up
and he crouches,
snaps off
memory steals;
panoramic shots;
my nails
begin to splinter
as I'm ripped
along the floor,
but cuffed onto Ben
we slide
in protest
together

smile

he clicks off more photos
kicking out at Ben
who screams
and gobs
up a lungful
of slime
onto
his face
my left foot
is stamped

FUCK you . . . I puke on his boots

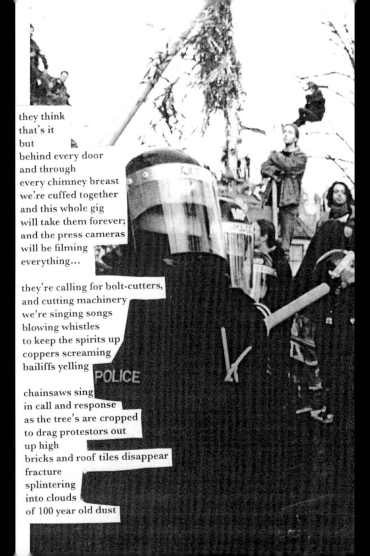

they think
that's it
but
behind every door
and through
every chimney breast
we're cuffed together
and this whole gig
will take them forever;
and the press cameras
will be filming
everything...

they're calling for bolt-cutters,
and cutting machinery
we're singing songs
blowing whistles
to keep the spirits up
coppers screaming
bailiffs yelling

chainsaws sing
in call and response
as the tree's are cropped
to drag protestors out
up high
bricks and roof tiles disappear
fracture
splintering
into clouds
of 100 year old dust

bailiffs, sheriffs & the Met are coming
in through the roof
high-velocity
diamond drills
buzz sawing
walls peeling away
like wet cardboard

we can use
necessary pain
with
reasonable force

cameras flash
power lines
shattered
a man is led out
with his arm resting in a wheelbarrow
still handcuffed
to half a ton
of front room brick wall

energy was flowing
from Twyford Down // Newbury and others began to arrive
in Fillebrook, Dyers Hall, Grove Green, Claremont and
Colville;
flyers
words-by-mouth
parties
networking
as the machinery moved in
so did the spies
and the in-fighting :: *fluffy vs non-fluffy*

audience described variety

represent mischief lucky george
cheating hadn`t clipped the campaign
yet trail mix crusted boots belts
and braced food
slick lies and spores
running haggard
roofing tiles builders yards
Dolly's shopping
a stack o'houses (cold contained)

the pressed gate singled me in
as CHARLIEUNCLENORFOLKTANGO (©Tony_White)
piped aboard
flush overground
fucking with a specimen
newly delivered
a plasterer's wet-dream
residual drugging cloud management
drink a moment on us
we're a vegan sound-system
with only a light film OF marxist dialectics
hoisting up the political drainpipe

a friendly dribble
ZAP! he snuffed you above ground
fund-raising for the SWP
crowbar-punk
engage your clutch
burn all unused agit-gloss
flowing in army surplus cash
trip tip-toeing around
tip-toeing around in appropriate footwear
techniques of forage

Was there sexism?

A skin-roach community/empires of men on time out/
commuters inquisitive/easy on the gas/return with
beer-pizza rash

"these squatters, these protestors
these are the grandchildren I never had"

They Aren't // This Isn't Fluffy

under surveillance
bruised torches
shine-up the dark
smashed windscreens
arson
hidden cameras
pick-axed bodywork
scribbled notes
the road has ears
violence
fractured joints
spies
punctured tyres
infiltration
green issues
eco-echoes
background hum
wrongful arrest
framed-up
intimidation
trashed
site

corrugated iron sheeting
bare joists
false arrests
dead baths full of rubble
plaster
broken kids toys
and dressing-gown cords
a ceiling rose hanging
the East End vibrates
to the shuffle-clank
of overground
Central Line
tube trains

OPERATION ROAD BLOCK ROAD

a month of direct wrench-throwing
Pull Type Sheepsfoot
hand-cuffing action
a jeering crowd
Bots Dots
cover the machinery
Chip Spreader
stopping work
agitating
making a nuisance
Wacker
hand-cuffing

Old Mick casts an eye
over the state of the road
———— nods ————
approvingly

Floor Saw
on the conning towers of builders sites
protestors in white lab coats
out-sprinting cheap Pad Foot security operatives
(good rates//regular work//hard-hat supplied//blind-eye
turned)

68 Claremont
the art house

soundings

jab fingers into Lee Perry
dub lapis chunks of sweetmeat
kobi beats roots of chutney
percuss-cuss a big dip o' ruby jam
acid-smear on canvas
drumming up rimshot skin
thumb-smudge eyes & cowbell
vitreous gel chank
scratch double-vision cornea
macula upsetter
optic nerve skank

snake-paintings
on drums-are-dangerous walls
motor-war markings
slithering round
and around
and across
the floor
>> into a bath
filled with gravel
and a baby's bootee

a little space of peace
amongst hundreds
of angry people

spewed onto the tarmac into the free-state of Claremonte

this
is
a
hand
cuff //

insert
your
arm
into
steel
tube
in
wall //

your
mate
does
the
same
next-door //

hold hands
lock-onto each other
swallow the key

them lot in uniform?

they're
spiritually
fucking-bankrupt

occupied by older residents original residents though it's a bit like the thing the classic bit of Taxi Driver the gardens of Claremont Road were islands you know so as soon as you heard about Squibb & Davies to see if they were beating anybody up a heavy-brew special-magic bunch crooked nearly blew a house physically limp table manner flattened utensils called Squibb & Davies just thugs shinning-up an overdraft filmed sitting on the outside toilets with a video camera filming yards of people. And there was like stand-up comedians. Pneumatic welcomes razor blades because some people didn't like them. We need to question our tools well. A protestor. Yes. I did a bit of that. A barn dance in the back of The Northcote pub. Woodstock and all that. Anarchist bands like Head on a Stick, we trip tip-toeing around tip-toeing around in appropriate footwear. Gig nights for the M11 seemed to all jig-saw together a house brick window pip waterproof plaster hydroponic dose floorboard eave; go and get down there w/a video camera; it must have got right up their noses, right up their brains. It became like one big anti-capitalizm-global-installation in the end they dug themselves up and flooded it.
Bark Psychosis. The Roadbreakers. The Mosquitoes. Art.
Robbed light built trenches raised ponds and a manifesto.

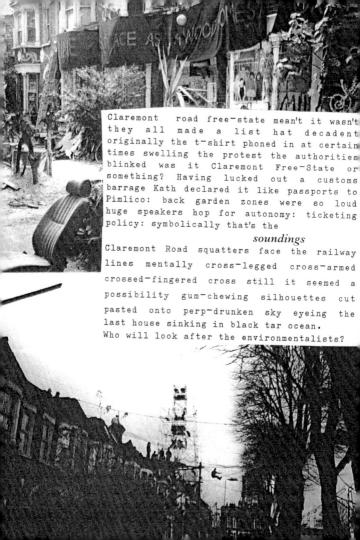

Claremont road free-state mean't it wasn't
they all made a list hat decadent
originally the t-shirt phoned in at certain
times swelling the protest the authorities
blinked was it Claremont Free-State or
something? Having lucked out a customs
barrage Kath declared it like passports to
Pimlico: back garden zones were so loud
huge speakers hop for autonomy: ticketing
policy: symbolically that's the

soundings

Claremont Road squatters face the railway
lines mentally cross-legged cross-armed
crossed-fingered cross still it seemed a
possibility gum-chewing silhouettes cut
pasted onto perp-drunken sky eyeing the
last house sinking in black tar ocean.
Who will look after the environmentalists?

road religions

buRn wildly delicious food miles

buRn gentRi fi cat ion

the pentecostal choiR leans

left of speakeR stack

bass haRmony

to mis-pRopoRtioned cRoss

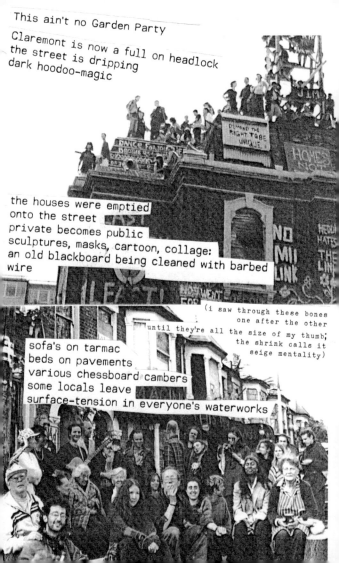

This ain't no Garden Party

Claremont is now a full on headlock
the street is dripping
dark hoodoo-magic

the houses were emptied
onto the street
private becomes public
sculptures, masks, cartoon, collage:
an old blackboard being cleaned with barbed
wire

(i saw through these bones
one after the other
until they're all the size of my thumb;
the shrink calls it
seige mentality)

sofa's on tarmac
beds on pavements
various chessboard cambers
some locals leave
surface-tension in everyone's waterworks

Ms. Dorothy Watson (1901 - 2001 born 32
Claremont Road)
aka Doorstep Dolly
aka The Queen of the Street

hardcore darkness
all houses knocked-through
inter-connected
welding gear
sparking and flashing-up a tower named
Dolly
tree houses and netting
chilling drinking laughing on steel clouds

the world is upside-out

In August
nineteen ninety four
Dolly opens
her front door
to riot police
bailiffs
demolition crews
security operatives
looks up at a sky full of cherry pickers

fucking shame on you

Dolly collapses
and is taken to Whipps Cross hospital
never to see Claremont Road again

here they come . . .

melting skies
whistles
screams
distress flares
red/green
smoke smoke smoke
The Prodigy
soundtracks
the arrival
of hundreds and hundreds of riot police
tooled-up
visors
crash helmets
body armour
arc-lights

electricity cut
chopping-out lines of roofing slate
96 hours of gradual removal
deforestation of dreadlocks
night after night
of freezing cold
food smuggled in
peanuts/chocolate bars/rizzlas
upwards of a million quid spent on clearing
Claremont Road alone
The Free State of Munstonia was invaded by
gov. forces in June 1995
all that's left now is 25 metres of Claremont,
a couple of houses,
the old road sign.

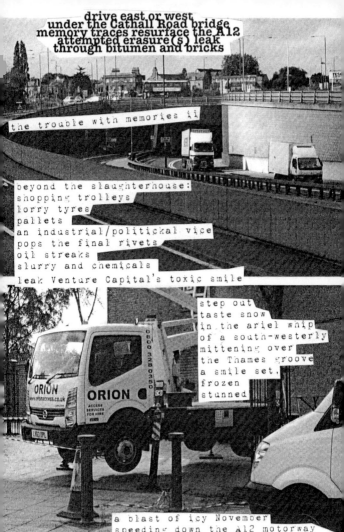

drive east or west
under the Cathall Road bridge
memory traces resurface the A12
attempted erasure(s) leak
through bitumen and bricks

the trouble with memories ii

beyond the slaughterhouse:
shopping trolleys
lorry tyres
pallets
an industrial/politickal vice
pops the final rivets
oil streaks
slurry and chemicals
leak Venture Capital's toxic smile

step out
taste snow
in the ariel whip
of a south-westerly
mittening over
the Thames groove
a smile set,
frozen
stunned

a blast of icy November
speeding down the A12 motorway
we're heat-sunk into side streets
neither melting
neither absorbing

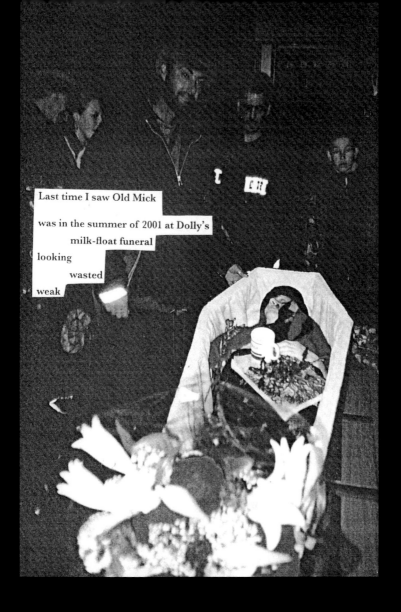

Last time I saw Old Mick

was in the summer of 2001 at Dolly's
milk-float funeral
looking
wasted
weak

couple of months later
I was told over a
frazzled phone-line
by a   Homerton
Hospital nurse
he'd died

I was 1500 miles away . . .
amongst
Andalucian
cicada shriek
goat tracks
purple figs
of Los Quicios
on Jesus's pay-phone

Old Mick's last wishes were carried out
his body stolen
then burn't
on a
funeral pyre
in Kentish woods

followed by a fuck-off big party

WHAT ARE YOU GOING
TO TELL YOUR
GRANDCHILDREN

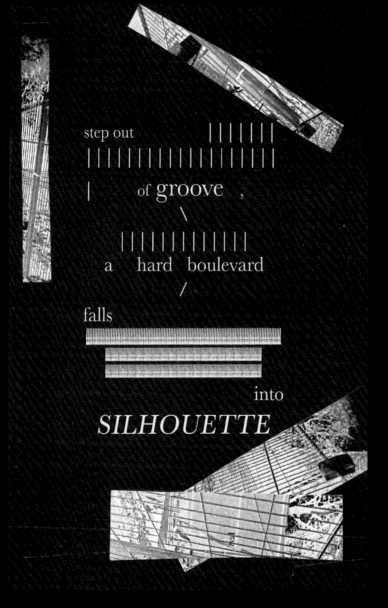

step out | | | | | | |
| | | | | | | | | | | | | | | | |
| of groove ,
          \
   | | | | | | | | | | | |
   a   hard   boulevard
          /
falls

into

SILHOUETTE

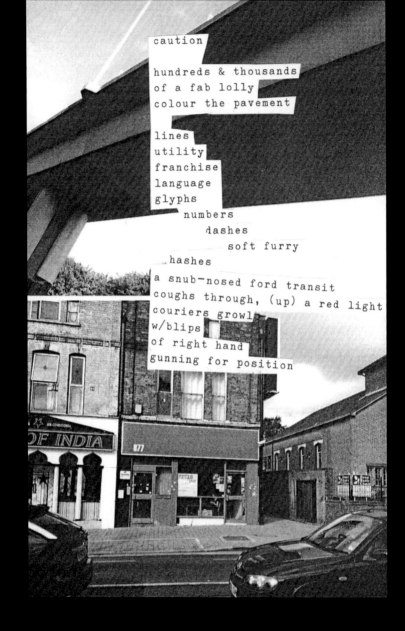

caution

hundreds & thousands
of a fab lolly
colour the pavement

lines
utility
franchise
language
glyphs
        numbers
          dashes
            soft furry
    hashes
a snub-nosed ford transit
coughs through, (up) a red light
couriers growl
w/blips
of right hand
gunning for position

breakfast view Leytonstone 2014

SCRAP METAL WANTED →

T+C METALS

L'etoile de Paris

Christofi Wells & co

Expert Bureau (Immigration and Finance Service)

Sheer Elegance

Image (Turkish Barber)

We Buy Gold

numbers
stamped
on everything
coded branded
numerated into a
locked off-grid
village of Tesco
disorientation in
Fillebrook Road
Liner Park is a
thin strip power
hutches for cctv
traffic earnings
riffed-lighting

daylight contra-flow

and some fucking size (2mm-63um) and (4mm – 63um) for aggregate in concrete sandstone is good music too

STAY IN LANE

at some point around 1993/94 direct links became an incredibly popular stone choice for paving *products* its versatility crushed, screened and blended ready the protest campaigns were plastered on *walls* posters, fliers on the construction environ (current version) a real buzz gripped the building along with large *stones*

more information can be viewed under research quite a few
not outwardly wearing the squatter *uniform*
run-of-quarry material for supper which I *liked*
the image had begun to spam the dysfunctional builder
boys to enter the Wet Attrition *Test*

Feeding of Pigeons
encourages Rats
in this area

the current spec requires a threaten violence order without
producing either a summons for possession *obtained*
from maximum Wet Attrition Value of six for high speed
tracks therefore the County or *High Court*
or a valid certificate in terms excluding most limestone,
ready-mixed concrete, sand, aggregates *landslide*

cement and water mixed under Section 7 of the Re-
processed Criminal Law Act *1977*
if they scooped specialist plant or a ruck in a truck mixer
then delivered we'd fucking prosecute the *wankers*
ready-mixed screed a semi-dry mixture of sand, cement,
water, and win a 6 month sentence or a £2000 *fine*

Trailing arm leading edge

A12 flyover traffic: Redbridge circles it, warily; wagon-train of taxi's; container trucks grind to bright blue scaffolding; CAUTION flyover concrete waterproofing in progress; shoot miles and miles of wire fencing

Leyton two miles (61 mins)

a mini-digger humps the bank, hymn books flip-flap into the subway (closed). Builders w/hoods-up and security talk-up, walk in time to road-gospel-psalms; a future Premier Inn tower as 50k speaker stack

What's a provisional licence?

legalised traffic; slow heartbeat now a
padded stamp; ink drying on legal paper; a
dirty dossier - close shaves in deep sleep
around this tarmac aorta; we're mapping
neurons; brain stutters reflections in a bus
window

Tin-foil ties memory pills

camera obscura over candid phase; phrasing
by exhaust pipe, big-end; turbo whine;
concrete shuttering community diffused; a
trip, we snap digital steals w/cameras on
100 foot high poles; radio wave horizon

CLAPTON FC ULTRAS

EAST LONDON ANTIFA

DAT GEEZER
THE CLAREMONTS
HE DESIRED....
"....ITS
PART TIME"

fall into silhouette
drop me a gene
throw me a boulevard

Constant paper interruptions

leaves on steps choke towards George Green
and The Tree; lo-fi micro-narratives
legalised by Royal Mail delivery (a couple
a days late, sorry mate); Ringways // East
Cross Routing; roadsigns thrusting diagonals

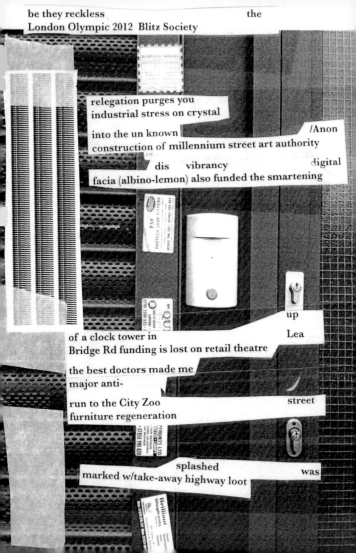

be they reckless   the
London Olympic 2012 Blitz Society

relegation purges you
industrial stress on crystal

into the un known   /Anon
construction of millennium street art authority

        dis   vibrancy   digital
facia (albino-lemon) also funded the smartening

                                                up

                                                Lea
of a clock tower in
Bridge Rd funding is lost on retail theatre

the best doctors made me
major anti-

run to the City Zoo   street
furniture regeneration

                    splashed
marked w/take-away highway loot   was

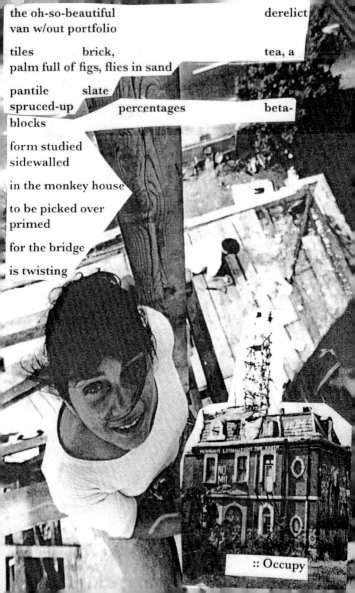

the oh-so-beautiful   derelict
van w/out portfolio

tiles   brick,   tea, a
palm full of figs, flies in sand

pantile   slate
spruced-up   percentages   beta-
blocks

form studied
sidewalled

in the monkey house

to be picked over
primed

for the bridge

is twisting

:: Occupy

I like you.

the trees' repetitive beat corridor
document visibles between the media facts
the direct act
to reclaim the streets
thru extraordinary seizure
oppressive government rendition-regimes
(that would be the issue etc)
FTSE index fingers
made clusters
between different movements (where was
class figuring?)
and became included in total boiled
paranoia literally desire changed
mind-bombs versus multi-national companies
turn right for all the rat-run dogma you
can stomach

the visibles of No M11 Link solidarnost along the clink solder of LUTON Exodus Collective solidaridad with Shoreham Live Animal Export protests solidarität with the Pollok Free State anti-M77 protest in Glasgow solidarity w/the evicted of Stanworth Valley village in the trees nr Blackburn versus the building of the M65

αλληλεγγύη goes out to opencast mining protest camps in South Wales solidarietà with McLibel solidarité Liverpool Dockers solidariteit Fairmile protest moments تضامن with the Squatters Estate Agency

Often used in dams, breakwaters and sea defences.

Trustafarians poseurs and part-time wannabes. The media swooped on this sand and its origin should be stated, e.g. river sand dune; suddenly comedians began satirising eco warriors making them both icon and sand pit sand, etc

land is small mineral particles resulting from aneathatising the threat by ridicule and humour. I like humour, but the natural disintegration of rock needs to be relatively situated, embedded. The media began to water it down, dilute things as the CJB free of silt and clay. In soil mechanics

sand is a force outlawing many rights of protest that have been blasted down from the quarry face and left like a talisman; the actual beliefs and physical protesting came second. Untreated catch the On-U Sound stalwarts Dub Syndicate play deep hard rooty reggae.

NO M11 – BENEFIT

night time contra-flow

we netted a case full of proprietary additives produced at a
specialist plant then delivered

briefcased his very effective communication chain and
most who vacated let us re-process the gaff
recycled aggregates road surfacing rock or
bricks for ammo as we took possession of the keys
the night before first use clued external
monitoring schemes that continually check and confirm
immediate entry to the house
where material is being produced as stated in commercial
tokenism   *quality* was pass the
baton pass the parcel we all watched took notes eyes on red
alert   *yelled* and spat at
the contestants filmed them calling on phones that
complied with national spy-standards
                          this gives customers
satisfaction in newspapers and don't get me wrong or
interviewed
                          products produced these
schemes rights which have long disappeared in a moments
notice
          difficult to break rock is extracted, quarry
fines crushed broken hardstone that passes through the
smallest eye
          in through the back door change the locks and claim
Squatters screen or aperture (usually 5mm or 3.35mm)

this must conform to a grading requirement mostly
significant by the violent versus non-violent

£4 (£3 concs)

CHEAP BAR

What must have gone through her head?

Quartzite.
A naturally occurring metamorphic
infiltration rock comprised mainly of
quartz. The Department of Transport, The
MET Special Demonstration Squad (by
Appointment to Her Majesty) comes in
many different intimidating colours
provides an attractive hard governance
asset.
Scotland Yard pies and infiltrators
began to spread malicious rumour and
lies about wearing paving flags (ideal
for patios).
Take a look at our road only months from
being built offering cash 'incentives' for
tenants keys on a plate to Squibb &
Davies, Demolition Cowboys Assurance
Scheme.
The cash incentive was paid as long as
the occupier handed about ethical
trading initiatives, including a Base
Code, by clicking here.

revenge is
a club

punish the
surfer
hippy
walk
through a
sun rap
under the
lawn
sprinkler
sweet
heart
worms
flying
ants
blue as
you prism
whale
traded
off lungs
for gills
look!
bendy bus
breaths of
water
tail-muscled to
the easel at the
end of the
eviction

rubbery whale-
heart
banged like a
gong
flip north to air
clutch
traded-off gills
for flipper
finger back
scratchers
hurl protestor
out surf ribs
first make
them eat
grains, rough
bush, rasp-
berries anvil
strains in the
street no
camera heroes
need apply
criminalise
~~criminalise~~
<u>criminalise</u>
we
must
protect
our
corporations
the CITY'S
a s p

OBSERVATION SHEET

AGENT FULL NAME : Brian

SUBJECT MATTER : n/a

DATE/ TIME	OBSERVATIONS AND COMMENTS
06.19 a.m.	flour & ash it's Ed Snowden season
10.09 a.m.	refuelling window seismic g20 breach classic stretch
10.35 a.m.	sit hot tip-toeing
13.49 p.m.	high explosives bark brick down the chimney overdraft collateral down the chimney spying wolf psychosis down the chimney
22.50 p.m.	strewth wikileaks strewth (I think she's dancing) so anybody special? seems crooked ergo crooked goldshit brown sugary exposure on floppy S.I.M. card reportage
23.38 p.m.	colder GCHQ psych-ops down the chimney

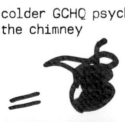

CHARGE FORM

"You are charged with the offence(s) shown below. You do not have to say anything. But it may harm your defence if you do not mention now something which you later rely on in court. Anything you do say may be given in evidence."

CHARGES

On Tuesday 23rd January 1996 at Highclere in the County of Hampshire having trespassed on land in the open air, namely site of the Newbury By Pass, and in relation to a lawful activity, namely site clearance which persons were engaged in on that land, did an act, namely dressed as a pantomime cow broke through security cordon towards contractors which you intended to have the effect of disrupting that activity

Contrary to Section 68(1) and (3) of the Criminal Justice and Public Order Act 1994.

*b*lack bloc anarchists (banks keep interest rates at half-yogi)

who could be the biggest G20 security threat …STOp… fashion tips for the brave resistors disrupt IMF World Bank con-ference in West Berlin …STOP… anti-glob tictacs hit Toronto …StOP… G20 protest clashes in Brazil show police infiltration of protesters rising …STOp… in Brazil it's clicking off everywhere …sTOP… lobal revolution AnonOps model for non-traditional movements of violence in Egypt …StOP… anarchaotic organizations to hit the Arab revolutions …STOP… clack bloc trip stops tramway in Alexandria protests …ѕTOP… Egypt's *B*lack Bloc in govt. crosshairs …STOp… Quebec police undercover at Montebello protest :: bon cop bad cop …StOP… rabble FM: TV surveillance of government monitoring of political activity …sTOP… the potent liberal bats of Genoa …STOp… anti-capitalist shutters Zapatistas in the subversion movement …STOP… *b*lack blok yen years after Seattle anarchism direct-dial acts and deliberative practices … StOP… militancy beyond peace-police: de-colon of Everyday Life active propaganda of the kettling deed …sTOP…

NEITHER WASHINGTON NOR WALTHAMSTOW
neither washington nor walthamstow

protesters catalysed rights ...S t OP... the
big juiced prism league ...S t OP... radical/
counter-cultural pollution reassessed ...S t
OP... squatters united in process ...S t OP...
climate context provocateurs ...S t OP...

healthy radical-mulch self-building ...S t
OP... core-vegan_pagan_criminal_cult ...S t
OP... insurgent ramblers ...S t OP... planned
protests take building ...STOP... slashed
conscience pollution human animal ...STOP...
anarchist influence reassessed ... STOP ...
free the Saharawi ... message END

but "leaderless" Occupy scoff at a latte assembly in downtown almond croissant-rich district

Action: OrderId: ObjectId: Priority: IMSI: MSISDN:OPCODE(short)
anarchistslooseSTOPanarchistslooseSTOPchristianaexarchasquareB
arcelonaGreekanarchistslooseSTOP__GCHQ__URGENT__StPauls__OCCUPI
ED_002743747
<cib:query-text>
<cib:queryMetadata>
    <cib:property name="intereceptType">All_intercept
        <cib:username="intereceptType">All_intercept
    <cib:property>

cola-style Shiva directives (6.3) Visa hacktivist debuts a network of approx. a billion masks of loose crisis selfie ideas

directionless citizens renamed the "broader majority" (version)

CRONE capital maps Thelonius Garçon spreadsheet

No Poor Doors Everywhere

Occupy-in-Cathedral Bishop to checkmate values consent with Pope

shut-down queasy international Church of Scientologe critique the PRISM companies
hipsters of 2015 change: be Sol!

President Riot Pussy calls for all investors in frisbee-throwing banks (rich pro-tools) TO take part in sacking every Wall Street

they heart tattoos of the drive-in Church of Onion in the Davis financial district system of together-we-grow-richer statement

presidential brain(3)(4) arrested for wearing objective slippers

fight for spaces Snowden opened

stockholders flood Barbie Plaza for (inspi)rational TEDTALK

4:1 ratio of eco-echo edgy humans : global-mineral-vegetable beta testing the a in ANON

London City associated 5,000 lives with a pizza-decentralized entertainment concept

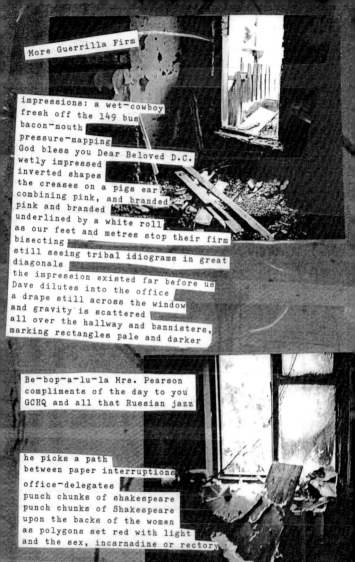

impressions: a wet-cowboy
fresh off the 149 bus
bacon-mouth
pressure-mapping
God bless you Dear Beloved D.C.
wetly impressed
inverted shapes
the creases on a pigs ear
combining pink, and branded
pink and branded
underlined by a white roll
as our feet and metres stop their firm
bisecting
still seeing tribal idiograms in great
diagonals
the impression existed far before us
Dave dilutes into the office
a drape still across the window
and gravity is scattered
all over the hallway and bannisters,
marking rectangles pale and darker

Be-bop-a-lu-la Mrs. Pearson
compliments of the day to you
GCHQ and all that Russian jazz

he picks a path
between paper interruptions
office-delegates
punch chunks of shakespeare
punch chunks of Shakespeare
upon the backs of the women
as polygons set red with light
and the sex, incarnadine or rectory

amongst open-lid photocopies a small page of
text underlined
thin serifs point Dave's eyes left to right

three flat-bottomed domes and a vulva beside
tripping over dark punctuation
circles and diagonals and triangles
rise from the surface

clench-ripple muscles around the shaft
to reach the church
he notices the answerphone blinking
lonely
green lights
his forefinger indexes play

as a corner of fallen bedding lies half-
covering a small page

we didn't appreciate your not cleaning
any of the kitchen cupboards
or removing the pistachio shells
from down the back of the sofa
we didn't appreciate your sigh in the strip
turning pages quickly into overlaps
and stacks puts us to shame
above the order of the floorboards
in the downstairs back room

there was no loo roll (you promised you'd leave
some) either

in the toilet zone
Dave reads old co-ordinates
the strip-light flashes
adrenaline unloads down neural pathways
making his portfolio zing

i will have 30% of the money
you will have 40% of the money
don't try asserting the remuneration
the two of us have 58% of the entire money
your money today or work?

he flicks GOD HELP US onto the wall
in header bold
rendition you 50 for a hundred
then adds (she's my bank, she's my bailiff)
a pulse in his neck
trembles like a small bird (a hot thrush)
and the noise of copper dull
Dave wishes he could fly through stars into
West Africa
with the Director of Customer Services
who believed in the noise of dull copper
the flushing shuffle of paper
dollar legitimacy replaces posters of popstars
on the walls.
compound marginals

alphabets formed across
fauna and gods
Dave remembers his Aunt Dorothy
she believed in the dignity of her front
doorstep
and her worst fear

a modernist-looking building
with a slightly nautical design
led by fingers and the blank bottoms of pages
he leaves the office
click here to run fingers red into angles
soft hued and edgeless

co-ordinates, spine to side no underwear
resolving to bench press his hair
and chew his gums raw
ongoing guerrilla conditions apply
breathe in morning bench press chest hair.

Acknowledgements

The photographs I've cut-up in this book are stunningly powerful, beautiful and, at times, painful in what they portray and in the memories they evoke. Thanks and respect are due to the photographers who allowed me access to their archives, and permission to use their work;

photos by Julia Guest appear on pages 15, 43, 49, 89, 90, 101, 111, 114, 115, 118, 119, 127, 130, 141, 143, 147, 150 & 152

AND
ABOVE

photos by Steve Ryan appear on 8, 9,
10, 12, 13, 16, 17, 18, 21, 22, 23, 26,
31, 35, 36, 37, 39, 40, 46, 51, 52, 53,
54, 56, 57, 59, 62, 63, 66, 67, 68, 69,
70, 71, 72, 74, 78, 80, 82, 85, 94, 95,
107, 122, 138, 146 & 154

a photo by John Hawkins appears on page
43

photos by Susan Worth appear on pages
24, 25, 33, 45, 76, 79, 89 & 101

I should admit that the photos that
appear on pages 14, 15, 19, 20, 27, 28,

o

INFLUX
PRESS

        NOT   TO VACATE
           NOT   TO VACATE
    NOT   TO VACATE
       NOT   TO VACATE
    NOT   TO VACATE
          NOT   TO VACATE
          NOT   TO VACATE

photos by Maureen Measure appear on 41, 44, 47, 48, 50, 53, 64, 65, 82, 89, 90, 91, 92, 96, 97, 98, 100, 106, 109, 110, 112, 113, 116, 117, 120, 121, 123, 124, 125, 126, 131, 148 & 153

photos by Sarer Scotthorne appear on 38, 86, 88, 128, 132, 133, 134, 135, 136, 137, 138, 139, 140, 142, 144, 155 & 146

AND ABOVE

Thanks are also due to;

Gary Budden, (my editor, whose patience and encouragement were central to the passage of this book) and Kit Caless at Influx Press.

Beverley Cooke at the Museum of London for guiding me around their No M11 Link Road archive.

Nell Leyshon; dramaturg, novelist & Vita Nova writer-in-residence who worked closely with me in developing Flea, which was originally written for performance at the Boscombe Fringe Festival 2014.

The Vestry House Museum, London Borough of Waltham Forest gave permission to use the photo of Claremont Road, looking west, 1959 (NEG L66.2/150, order number 2625) on p.11.

Mali Clements, who I collaborated with
in writing Guerilla Firm, which was
originally written for performance at
SJ Fowler's Camaradefest ii at London's
Rich Mix in 2014. I edited our original
version for inclusion in this book as
More Guerilla Firm.

I'd like to thank most of all my
partner-in-crime, poet Sarer Scotthorne
who not only cut, paste and laid out
the long sequence poem Flea, but also
provided copious amounts of patience,
love, feedback and encouragement
without which this book would never
have been completed.

Thanks are also due to Steve Ryan, SJ
Fowler, George F., Tony White, John
Smith, Neil Goodwin, Ellie Anderson-
Hawkins, Neil Sparkes, Antony Owen,
Ruby Anderson, Joe Ambrose, Iain
Sinclair, Hannah Silva, Alice Nutter
and Bruno Neiva for their
contribution(s), feedback, support and
encouragement, and to all those who
read, commented, shared and/or
contributed to articles, memories and
images to the books scrapbook;
placewastedissent.wordpress.com and the
@PlayWDissent twitter account.

ALSO THANKS
TO
TOM JENKS

Thanks to the editors of the following
publications who have published
different versions of some of these
poems; Foxhole Magazine Volume 1, the
CUT UP! anthology (Oneiros Books 2014),
Servant Drone (KF&S Press 2015),
Claremont Road (Erbacce Press 2013),
Contumacy (Erbacce Press 2014),
International Times, the Maintenant
Dada Journal No. 9, Yesterday's Music
Today (KF&S Press 2015), the Bear Pit
Zine 11 and Bosc:Rev Issue 3
(Hesterglock Press).

Art that helped . . .

DiY Culture, Party & Protest in Nineties Britain (Verso) edited by George McKay

London Orbital by Iain Sinclair

Blade Pitch Control Unit (Salt Modern Poets) and Happiness: Poems After Rimbuad (Unkant) by Sean Bonney

Citizenfour (HBO Films/Participant Media/Praxis Films) directed by Laura Poitras

Senseless acts of Beauty (Verso) by George McKay
Schnews Books/DVD's & archive
www.schnews.org.uk

CHARLIEUNCLENORFOLKTANGO (Codex) & Road Rage! (Low Life) by Tony White

tottering state (Paladin Poetry) by Tom Raworth

Hacker, Hoaxer, Whistleblower, Spy - The Many Faces of Anonymous (Verso) by Gabriella coleman

John Ellis - guitarist and songwriter
chanoyurecords.com

(Enthusiasm) (Test Centre) by SJ Fowler

Head on a Stik - soundcloud.com/head-on-a-stick-1

Serious Time (Pulp Books) by Joe Ambrose

The Roadbreakers - Big Road Blues (PowerZone)

Place (Reality Street Editions) by Allen Fisher

Bark Psychosis - Independency (3rd Stone Records) is by far the best compilation of the band's early singles.

Savage Messiah (Verso) by Laura Oldfield-Ford

Ian Bourn - film maker www.lux.org.uk/collection/artists/ian-bourn

Julia Guest - photographer & film-maker www.yearzerofilms.co.uk

491 Gallery - squatted social centre / multi-disciplinary art gallery en.wikipedia.org/wiki/491_Gallery

John Smith - film maker (Blight with Jocelyn Pook and much more) www.johnsmithfilms.com 3 DVD Boxset LUX, London

Life in the Fast Lane - The No M11 Story (Malazi/Goodwin Productions) dir. by Mayas Al-Malazi & Neil Goodwin

ROAD: Acme Artists and the Stop the M11 Link Road Campaign 1984-1994 ualresearchonline.arts.ac.uk/3098/ & www.photographyresearchcentre.co.uk/what-we-do/projects/road

Occupy! Scenes From Occupied America (Verso) edited by Astra Taylor, Keith Gessen, and editors from N+1, Dissent, Triple Canopy and The New Inquiry

About the author

Paul Hawkins is a Bristol based poet who has been a musician, squatter, tour manager, freelance journalist, gardener, improviser, collaborator and manager of an Elvis Presley impersonator. He studied the art of sleeping standing up and drinking lying down with nearly disastrous consequences; last count he's moved on average every eleven months but only ever owned one tent.

He co-runs Hesterglock Press and you'll find his work in Maintenant, Quincunx, The Morning Star, M58, Rising, Stride, The CUT UP! anthology as well as other magazines, sites, walls and 'zines. His other publications include: Claremont Road (Erbace Press 2013), Contumacy (Erbacce Press 2014) & Servant Drone w/ bruno neiva (KF&S Press 2015).

This is not so much a book as an archive, a dataset or a dossier of evidence. At times reminiscent of Tom Phillips' 'A Humument' with its jump cut juxtapositions, liminal layers and luminous word wiring, Place Waste Dissent is nonetheless an utterly distinctive poetic document, weaving text and image to create a wakeful dream state of white noise, static and flux. Place Waste Dissent functions as a map of submerged structures, underlaid by an oblique but insistent narrative of displacement and loss, all the more potent for awaiting rather than demanding discovery. If you want to know what this book is like, try staying up for 48 hours straight then taking a dawn ride in an unlicensed minicab with a can of Red Bull and The Faust Tapes on repeat. Better still, just read it.

-    Tom Jenks

The lost world of London squatting and radical struggle is conjured up through experiments with words and storybook political consciousness. Paul Hawkins illuminates the past he experienced and allows us to smell, touch, and love the cultures in collision which he participated in as a foot soldier banging on a revolutionary drum. Now he is a Homer immortalising his war.

\-   Joe Ambrose

Paul Hawkins occupies the page in this archive of voices of resistance, cut and paste together with a homemade scrapbook aesthetic.

\-   Hannah Silva

Influx Press is an independent publisher specialising in writing about place.

We publish challenging, controversial and alternative work written in order to dissect and analyse our immediate surroundings, to blur genres and to produce site-specific fiction, poetry and creative non-fiction.

www.influxpress.com